CABIN LIVING

CABIN LIVING

DISCOVERING THE SIMPLE AMERICAN GETAWAY

The Editors of *Cabin Living* Magazine

Guilford, Connecticut

An imprint of Globe Pequot

Distributed by NATIONAL BOOK NETWORK

Copyright © 2018 ACTIVE INTEREST MEDIA

British Library Cataloguing in Publication Information available

Library of Congress Cataloging-in-Publication Data

Title: Cabin living : discovering the simple American getaway / the editors of *Cabin Living*.
Description: Guilford, Connecticut : Lyons Press, 2017. | Description based on print version record and CIP data provided by publisher; resource not viewed.
Identifiers: LCCN 2017016649 (print) | LCCN 2017018442 (ebook) | ISBN 9781493030446 (e-book) | ISBN 9781493030439 (pbk.)
Subjects: LCSH: Vacation homes—United States. | Log cabins—United States.
Classification: LCC NA7574 (ebook) | LCC NA7574 .C323 2017 (print) | DDC 728.7/30973—dc23
LC record available at https://lccn.loc.gov/2017016649

♾™ The paper used in this publication meets the minimum requirements of American National Standard for Information Sciences—Permanence of Paper for Printed Library Materials, ANSI/NISO Z39.48-1992.

Printed in the United States of America

TO THE LOYAL, LONGTIME SUBSCRIBERS TO *CABIN LIFE/CABIN LIVING* MAGAZINE:

Thank you for letting us into your special world. It has been our honor and pleasure to serve you over the past seventeen years. Here's to many more!

CONTENTS

INTRODUCTION

"I'D RATHER BE AT THE CABIN." That simple statement—which we first printed on bumper stickers sixteen years ago in the early days of *Cabin Life/Cabin Living* magazine—says it all. To this day, the bumper sticker has been wildly successful. Of course it has, because it perfectly sums up the passion America has for the cabin retreat lifestyle. For those times when you can't be at the cabin, you can get your "get-away-from-it-all" fix with this book. If you don't own a cabin yet, but you're dreaming of buying or building someday, this book's stories are an inspiring, resounding statement that achieving the dream is possible!

For many today, getting away from it all by escaping to a cabin is part of the great American dream. Cabin living is, indeed, foundational to the American way of life in terms of history, architecture and family culture. Starting in the eighteenth century, when Scandinavian and Scotch-Irish settlers built homes in America, a simple log cabin was often the structure of choice. The story on page 231, "Rebuilding a Pioneer Cabin," actually centers on such a cabin. A strong case can be made that the cabin is America's vernacular architecture. And the simple log cabin is the stuff of American legend and lore, the most iconic story being that of President Abraham Lincoln, who was born in a log cabin on his father's Kentucky farm. When you imagine a young Abe Lincoln, your mind picture is probably of him next to a wood pile, axe in hand, in front of the family cabin.

At some point in American history, the notion of a "cabin" evolved into something other than a rustic home, as the idea of a getaway retreat was born. Wealthy city dwellers wanted a place in the country they could escape to, leaving the summer heat of the city behind. Some of the most notable and architecturally significant retreats were the early-nineteenth-century Great Camps in the Adirondacks, owned by families with names like Vanderbilt and Rockefeller.

Eventually, the dream of a getaway retreat became accessible to the masses. Even my grandfather Art, the son of Danish immigrants who grew up during the Great Depression and achieved only an eighth-grade education, was able to buy a small lake cottage in northern Minnesota in the late 1950s. As the getaway dream flourished for families across America, people called their places by different names, and this is still true today. Depending on a person's background and where in the country their retreat is located, they might call their place a cabin, cottage, camp, country house or lake home. At *Cabin Life/Cabin Living* magazine, we have used all those words, but we prefer the collective term "cabin."

So what is a cabin? What people call their places varies, the style of construction and décor can be vastly different, and the sizes of the structures can deviate dramatically, but there are strong underlying themes. The cabin is a retreat for connecting with family, friends, and nature. It's even a place for reconnecting with the best part of ourselves that we may have lost touch with during the stress and grind of daily life back home. The cabin is a place to decompress; as you arrive and drive down the gravel driveway on a Friday night, you can feel your shoulders relax and your heart rate blissfully slow down.

This book consists of thirty stories of people who achieved their cabin living dream. (No, my Grandpa Art's cottage didn't make the cut.) These are Cabin Tour feature stories from the pages of *Cabin Life/Cabin Living* magazine. The heart and soul of the magazine, the Cabin Tour features are photo-driven, inspirational cabin owner success stories. The thirty stories in this book were chosen by our editors because they're the best, most inclusive and representative stories with stunning photography. You'll visit cabins across the United States, from Maine to Wisconsin to California and beyond.

The book is organized into sections that showcase new and aspirational cabins; how to get the most out of small cabins; renovated, made-over, and rebuilt cabins; retreats with fabulous outdoor living spaces; and finally cabins with a strong sense of history and family that have been passed down through the generations.

Here's wishing you more great times at the cabin,

—Mark R. Johnson
Editor in Chief, *Cabin Living* magazine

To subscribe to *Cabin Living* magazine, go to: www.CabinLivingMag.com/Subscribe.

ACKNOWLEDGMENTS

FIRST AND FOREMOST, to the loyal readers of *Cabin Life/Cabin Living* magazine: I am in your debt and at your service. Thank you to the founders who bravely struck out in the spring of 2001 to launch a national magazine for cabin owners and dreamers, especially chairman Lars Fladmark, publisher Toni Fladmark, editor Diana Faherty, and production manager Pat Kelley. And thanks, Toni and Diana, for hiring me a couple months later. Thanks to art/creative directors Tanya Nygren Back, Elizabeth M. Weber, and Edie Mann, who have made *Cabin Life/Cabin Living* soar! Thank you, publishers Linda Kast and Peter Miller, for your leadership. Thanks to the über-talented writers and photographers who contributed the fabulous Cabin Tour feature stories that make up this book and to Fran Sigurdsson for your exceptional copywriting services on this book project. Last, but definitely not least, thank you to my soul mate and wife, Carol, and sons Loren and Cole, who have supported and encouraged me during this wild seventeen-year ride.

THE DREAM CABIN

Dream cabin stories are inspirational, showing that the cabin dream is alive and well in America. Most of these cabin owners realized their dreams by building new retreats—some as weekend getaways, others for living out their golden retirement years. The stories in this section are also aspirational, as these are no ordinary structures. They include a dramatic rustic log retreat, a hybrid lake home, a modern hillside getaway, and two cabins designed with historic, vintage flair.

A cabin "up north" fits one Wisconsin couple perfectly.

"MANY DIFFERENT ELEMENTS WERE MIXED WITHIN TO GIVE IT ITS STRIKING APPEARANCE BUT COZY FEEL."

HEAVEN HAS A DOCK

Randy and Janelle Lang consider themselves "Northwoods people." Ever since Randy was a small boy, he's vacationed in northern Wisconsin. Taking in the beauty of dark pine forests reflected on clear lake waters, he forged a lasting bond with nature.

Janelle, who grew up in Milwaukee, was no stranger to cabin living "up north." The two met and settled in Wausau in north-central Wisconsin.

Three children and five grandchildren later, both Randy and Janelle were ready to retire from the engineering firm they owned. It was time to downsize. The couple decided to sell their home and a small getaway in the Northwoods. Instead, they would build a year-round retirement cabin a little farther north.

The Manitowish Chain O' Lakes was a natural choice for them. Randy had visited the area frequently with his parents. "We had a cabin for many years on a small lake by Mercer, which is just down the road. So we had roots in this area for many years," he explains.

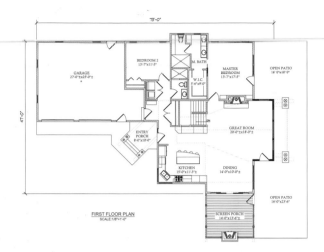

FIRST FLOOR PLAN
SCALE:1/8"=1'-0"

The Langs' property borders one of the ten lakes in the chain, and the land is mostly wooded. And they are right on the water, which they love. As things turned out, they couldn't be happier with their decision.

DESIGNING A DREAM

Originally, the Langs planned to build a traditional full log cabin. But the vision evolved as they studied log home magazines and clipped photos of elements they liked. Incorporating different features, the couple arrived at a unique design for their dream retreat.

After interviewing a number of builders, they clicked with Tomahawk Log & Country Homes outside Wausau. Sales manager and design consultant Troy Gullo worked with Randy and Janelle on their design. In the end, the Langs came up with about 90 percent of the design, with a few elements added by Tomahawk.

Their cabin is a hybrid form featuring plenty of wood, stone, and log accents inside and out. Tomahawk's patented construction system combines conventionally framed and insulated stud walls with handhewn, half-log sheathing and full log corners. "It has the timber-frame look in some areas, and the log look in certain areas," says Gullo. "Many different elements were mixed within to give it its striking appearance, but cozy feel."

MAKING A LIST

There were a few "must haves" for the Langs when building their permanent cabin. On the wish list: a lake view from the primary rooms. The great

Top: The Langs designed their one-floor home to remain comfortable for them as they age.

Bottom: Personal touches make the Langs' cabin truly one of a kind.

The great room is perfect for gathering family to enjoy a fire on a crisp fall day.

room, dining room, and kitchen are all open and look out to the lake. Plus, the master bedroom contains a number of windows on the lake side of the cabin. "It was real important to us that we had a lot of windows in the home," Janelle says. The large window grouping in the great room was Randy's idea and design.

The screened porch was essential, too. It gets used year-round. "When you live in the Northwoods, and you have mosquitoes in the summer, you need to have a screen porch," Janelle explains.

The couple also wanted wood-burning stone fireplaces in the great room and on the screened porch. In the cooler seasons, the fireplace makes the porch a favorite spot to sit and relax. (A lower-level fireplace is gas, so Randy and Janelle don't have to carry wood down the stairs.)

A stone backsplash behind the cooktop and hood adds an earthy texture to the kitchen.

Every season at the cabin brings special enjoyment for the Langs.

"Heaven has a dock."

PLANNING AHEAD

Since this was to be their retirement home, the Langs wanted to minimize square footage and live on one level. (They knew they would not want to be climbing a lot of stairs in the future.)

Once the main level was completed, they decided to finish off the basement for additional living space. Separating the project into two phases allowed them to plan better and to save money. A large family room with a fireplace and a guest bedroom were planned. Because the lot is very level, a walkout basement wasn't feasible. So enough ground near the cabin was removed to create a rock berm and install windows. "The berm areas are maybe fifteen feet square, rather than just window wells," Randy mentions. The windows provide emergency egress for the guest room and make the basement space more inviting.

The decorative ceiling in the bedroom is made of tin. The Langs chose this for looks but also for function, since it allows them to access the underside of the main-level floors. "I wanted it fully accessible," Randy says. "I didn't want to have it 'drywalled in.' We have minimal drywall in the house."

HANDS-ON HELP

With a background in construction as well as engineering, Randy performed all the wiring and electrical work himself. Wireless lighting controls that utilize radio-frequency signals activate dimming modules. The controls are completely programmable so any switch can control any light in the house.

Being on the job site on a regular basis also meant Randy was able to address any questions or concerns the builders had. His engineering skills were definitely beneficial, comments Troy Gullo.

8 TIPS FOR SITING YOUR DREAM CABIN

To properly site a retreat, cabin owners should:

- Verify access to utilities and whether the land is served by septic or sewer.
- Make the lay of the land a partner in their design.
- Allow trees, boulders, or other large elements to remain nearby for scale.
- Prioritize outdoor living spaces.
- Consider views across and through the site.
- Take advantage of shading deciduous trees to the south and west.
- Plot both summer and winter sunrises and sunsets on your plan.
- Open the cabin to eastern and southern exposures to admit natural light during the cooler part of the day.
- Consider surface and subsurface drainage, as well as seasonal/tidal variations in water levels and flood elevations.
- Isolate vehicle circulation to minimize intrusion into view corridors and outdoor living spaces.

"Someone as organized and thorough as Randy makes a project run a lot smoother because you know what he is looking for."

GOING WITH THE FLOW

Part of the fun of building a new home is making decisions on the interior design and décor. "We did a lot of looking, and we probably bought just about every log home/cabin magazine there was for about five years," Randy says. They also attended many log home shows for ideas.

The couple picked out all the wood and materials themselves. Pine was used throughout most of the home; interior walls are knotty pine. The flooring, with in-floor heating, is white oak with a burnished cherry finish. Certain finishes and accents were used throughout for consistency. "Probably one of the most difficult things was getting the colors right with the stain on the wood," Janelle says. "That's a little tricky, because when you look at a small sample of something, and then you look at it on a big surface, it doesn't always look the same." Different lighting can also affect the look, she notes.

Reclaimed materials weren't used in the build, but the flooring was stained and distressed to achieve a reclaimed look.

Another rustic touch is the twig chandelier Randy constructed for the great room, using alder branches harvested from a local swamp. Also in the great room above the fireplace are bifold doors covering a TV. "We made the bifold doors so that painted panels can be placed on the doors, creating a picture. The panels are removable, so we can have a painting for each season," Randy says.

Over time, and throughout their travels living the Northwoods lifestyle, the Langs collected stones from the shores of Lake Michigan and Lake Superior. As a personal touch, they added these stones to the showers in their cabin home.

LIFE ON THE LAKE

Summer is the time to be up here to enjoy the lake," Janelle says. The Langs don't miss out on the opportunities at their doorstep. Favorite warm weather activities include fishing, swimming, and riding the pontoon boat through the chain of lakes. "I can't think of a nicer way to enjoy the beauty of nature than sitting out on a dock overlooking the lake," says Janelle, "or watching the animals, or walking in the woods. It's just a very relaxed, comfortable lifestyle. I tell you, every day I'm thankful that I get to live in this beautiful place."

These days, it can be hard to get the entire family together, especially with the couple's daughter now living in California with three of their grandchildren. But everyone

The great room's view of the water is framed by a wall of windows accented with dark wood trim.

tries to come for the Fourth of July week—a prime time to visit, given the usually beautiful weather. Christmas is also a joyous occasion at the cabin.

When the snow flies, the Langs don snowshoes or go snowmobiling. "Up here, it is a winter wonderland," Janelle says. "Being in the Northwoods is fun at any time of the year." Until, that is, the temperatures turn frigid. During the coldest months, these snowbirds nest in the Florida Keys. But soon enough, they return to what Janelle calls their "little piece of heaven." Randy echoes the sentiment. "They do say," he remarks, "'heaven has a dock.'" ■

A special aspect of this handcrafted log home is the carved eagle under the overhang.

> **"WE WANTED TO MAKE THE CABIN UNIQUE AND RUSTIC BUT ALSO COMFORTABLE AND INVITING."**

A CABIN BUILT FOR RELAXATION

When Tom and Sue Jellison bought land in Three Rivers, Michigan, Tom had a simple plan. You might even say a "manly" plan: Build a log cabin and outfit it with a fireplace, bar, loft, and bunk beds. Period. Sue, Tom's wife, had a vision for a log home, one that included nice amenities.

"Yes, I wanted heat with running water!" Sue says with a smile. "I also envisioned bedrooms upstairs with bathrooms. I just wanted to make sure it felt more like a home than a hunting lodge." She also wanted to outfit the entire cabin with log furniture: headboards, dressers, nightstands, tables and chairs, stools, end tables, lamp stands, flower vases, and more.

In the end, the two minds came together on a plan. "We wanted to make the cabin unique and rustic but also comfortable and inviting," says Tom.

LOVE AT FIRST SIGHT—ON TV

Tom and Sue began researching the log-home industry and talking to different builders. Then one night, Tom was channel surfing when

Log-style barstools, chiseled-edge granite countertops, and a copper farm sink give touches of rustic elegance to the kitchen.

The pull of a rocking chair makes for guilt-free downtime.

something on HGTV caught his eye. It was a cabin built out of old-growth, tight-grained, western red cedar logs. With no caulking or chinking between logs, the airtight structure was reported to be impervious to mold, mildew, and insect infestation. Tom and Sue also learned that the home promised great acoustic ability for extra peace and quiet.

It was the striking look of the structure, however, that kept their eyes fixated on the television screen. The couple was mesmerized by the mammoth cedar logs, the tongue-and-groove construction, and the carefully handcrafted detail afforded to each log.

"It was just what we wanted," says Tom. "We were so impressed with the quality of the product and the master craftsmanship."

The cabin featured was built by Pioneer Log Homes Midwest in Grafton, Wisconsin. The Jellisons' search was over.

JUST A CHAIN SAW AND HAND TOOLS

Pioneer—along with John Howard, the local carpenter the Jellisons hired—erected a 2,300-square-foot structure using nothing but a chain saw and hand tools. The end result is a rustic, handcrafted log home with a master suite, two guest bedrooms, two-and-a-half baths, a large wet bar, and a loft with two sitting areas.

Tom and Sue didn't want any drywall in their cabin. Instead, they used tongue-and-groove cedar paneling for the walls, and walnut and stone floors throughout. The open floor plan helps to provide the lodge-like feel Tom wanted. Pine cabinets, log-style barstools, chiseled-edge granite countertops, and a copper farm sink lend rustic elegance to the kitchen. In the dining area, the Jellisons use two small wooden tables rather than one big one to make the room more spacious. (When they host

In the dining area, the Jellisons use two small wooden tables rather than one large one to make the room more spacious. The fireplace is made of natural river-rock fieldstone.

The hand-carved doors are made of Douglas fir.

This bathroom's custom wood sink is also handcrafted.

By night, Tom and Sue like to relax by the fire pit.

large groups, they push the tables together.) The fireplace is made of natural river-rock fieldstone.

CREATIVE CARVING

One of Pioneer's finishing touches is a custom woodcarving, usually positioned on a home's ridge beam. The Jellisons' majestic eagle, however, keeps a watchful eye on the back porch/pond side of the cabin, placed under the overhang for protection.

The firm's owner, John Leszczynski, also presented the couple with an unexpected treat: a built-in carved bench on the back porch. The Jellisons were thrilled. "Tom and Sue said that they planned to spend a lot of time on their porch," said Leszczynski. "So I figured they would appreciate the bench."

Tom and Sue used tongue-and-groove cedar paneling for the walls and walnut and stone floor throughout.

Sue planned a red and gold color scheme, so she found fabrics she liked and then special-ordered the furniture.

The cabin also includes two decks that wrap together, as well as several interior and exterior hand-carved doors made of Douglas fir. The intricate carvings—one of an elk surrounded by tall pines, one of a moose in a meadow, another of a bear in a stream with a fish in its mouth—add rustic appeal. Other special touches include bear tracks that appear on select logs and a hand-carved bathroom sink.

A PLACE TO UNWIND AND DE-STRESS

Tom, who owns and runs five companies, wanted a nice retreat where he could regularly host customers and vendors. He got his wish. "The place is ideal for entertaining business contacts. But it has also turned out to be a fantastic place for me to de-stress and decompress," says Tom.

The Jellisons' year-round home is just twenty-five miles away in Elkhart, Indiana. "I can leave the office and be to the cabin in less than thirty minutes. It's wonderful!" says Tom.

The Jellisons spend weekends and holidays at the cabin with family and friends, plus their eight-year-old shih apso dog, Emma. Their grown children, BJ and Paige, also relish cabin time. And who can blame them? The retreat sits on fifty acres of alfalfa fields, with ATV trails that surround the property.

The cabin also has a great view of their three-quarter-acre pond, which Tom keeps stocked with bluegill, largemouth bass, and perch. "My patience level is pretty short," says Tom with a chuckle. "So I want to always have enough fish in there so that I can cast out and catch something within two or three minutes."

Tom and Sue like to relax outside and sip coffee as they watch hummingbirds flutter and listen to wild turkeys gobbling. The property also offers a shooting range and plenty of woods for hunting. Sue's fondness for wildlife, however, has put a crimp in Tom's hunting.

"My wife will say, 'Don't shoot Albert!'" notes Tom. "I must admit, it's hard to hunt when she's named most of the deer!"

In lieu of grabbing his gun, Tom often grabs a drink and unwinds on the porch. "I'm not a person who can sit still for too long," says Tom. "But when I'm at the cabin, it's a different story."

The lure of a cozy rocking chair, a breathtaking sunset, a refreshing drink, and the gentle whisper of an afternoon breeze certainly make for guilt-free downtime. And that's something Tom never had enough of—until now.

"Building this place is the best thing I've ever done," says Tom. "Honestly, it has totally changed my life." ∎

This cabin boasts a twenty-mile view of the Great Craggy Mountains and the spruce-shrouded Black Mountains. The Blacks are the highest range in eastern North America.

HILLSIDE HEAVEN

Cabin life is truly a peak experience for Bill and Phyllis Malcolm. Perched at an elevation of 2,850 feet, their hillside heaven offers breathtaking views of the Blue Ridge Mountains. From their deck, the Malcolms can gaze across to the Craggies and Mount Mitchell—the highest peak east of the Mississippi.

GENESIS OF A DREAM

It all started with an invitation from one of Bill's business clients in the fall of 2005. Would the couple like to visit her retreat outside Boone, North Carolina? Call it serendipity. Destiny, even. Because earlier that week, Phyllis remarked to Bill how she would love to have a cabin in the woods.

The Malcolms drove up from Florida that November. These transplanted northerners—Bill is from Illinois, Phyllis hails from Ohio—met at college in Boca Raton. They married in 1980 and settled in the Boca vicinity. The couple often traversed the I-95 corridor through eastern North Carolina to visit family. But they had never ventured west to the Appalachians. When they finally did, it was love at first sight.

The kitchen island is the center of the cabin. Whoever is cooking at the range-top on the island can do so while engaging with guests and enjoying views.

This Hoosier cabinet sits in a hallway niche where it stores cookbooks and vintage kitchen items.

The two returned to western North Carolina the following May, determined to find their own aerie. They explored far and wide in order to get a feel for the area. "I put on 1,400 miles in four days," laughs Bill. On the Fourth of July, they pulled into Black Mountain, a small town just east of Asheville. "It's quaint, nice, with everything you could want," says Phyllis.

An Internet search led to a nearby mountain development. Creston Community features about 138 lots on 1,000-plus acres of forest land. Half the property is under conservation easements, crisscrossed by streams and hiking trails. "When you come through the main gate, it's a three-mile ride around the mountain and up to the top," says Bill. "You've got privacy." Yet Black Mountain is only twenty minutes away, satisfying the couple's desire for close-by amenities. Asheville, an arts mecca, is another twenty minutes farther. And the local recreational opportunities are virtually unlimited.

Blending materials adds visual interest to this bathroom.

Red oak flooring unifies the interior, while different ceiling heights and floor treatments delineate areas by function.

Including fairies in gardens is part of mountain tradition.

PLANNING

In September, the Malcolms purchased a north-facing lot for its spectacular long-range vistas.

But what type of cabin should they build? They mulled over timber-frame packages before approaching Black Mountain architect Thomas Lawton. "Tom was already up here on the mountain," notes Bill. "He designed for the lady who lives above us. We were there and liked it."

The couple wanted a bright, breezy retreat that embraced the outdoors. They also wanted to "ground" their tree house with natural stone and wood. For both, memories of idyllic childhood summers served as inspiration. Phyllis recalls family outings at a great-uncle's wooded retreat in Brunswick, Ohio. And Bill's folks owned a cottage on the Kankakee River near Joliet, Illinois, where the clan boated and fished.

After evaluating the site, Lawton proposed an out-of-the-box approach. "The big design challenge was the steepness of the site and having access on the south while the view was to the north," he says.

Just as the couple went to contract in September 2008, the financial world collapsed. "Suddenly, everything was up in the air," Bill recalls. The project floated for three years before the Malcolms were ready to commit.

Once they were ready, hiring the right builder was crucial since they could make only occasional site visits. A neighbor introduced Randy Hughes of Blue Ridge Mountain Homes. "After fifteen minutes," recalls Bill, "I said, 'You're my man.' Randy is meticulous, with a great eye for detail."

Construction finally commenced. But first, several feet of unsuitable soil (non-compactible tree roots and undergrowth) had to be removed before a deep concrete foundation could be poured. Cutting into a hill also required a concrete retaining wall.

BUILDING AN AERIE?

Keep in mind that:

- Construction costs on a steep lot can soar without proper planning, most notably in the foundation. A narrow footprint can help—less material will be needed—while still providing great views.
- You don't always need to go quite as big on upper levels if there's room for living space on the lower level. Basement projects are great to consider for expansion, especially for more sleeping space.
- If the slope allows the lower level to be exposed, add windows and a door to create a walkout basement. Not only does a walkout provide full access to the property, it also increases your cabin's value.

An abundance of windows makes for bright and cheery spaces.

The cabin is tucked into the slope, with three levels that hug the hill's contours. A daylight (walk-out) basement sits on a slab on grade. An office here allows Bill to work while he transitions into retirement. Both office and adjoining exercise room open onto a terrace.

LONG AND LINEAR

The main level accounts for over half of the cabin's square footage. A long, linear floor plan with the dining room at one end and a master suite at the other maximizes the narrow site. A cantilevered living room "telescopes" off the kitchen to capture the view. Approximately 1,000 square feet of dining porch and deck extend the living space as much as possible.

Large casement windows drench the cabin in light and afford glimpses of wildlife. Flocks of turkeys cut across the slope below, and droves of hummingbirds are a common sight. At least, they were before the Malcolms noticed that bird feeders also attract bears in these parts. (They lost two feeders before strapping a third to the edge of the deck. Undeterred, a bear jumped onto the railing and snatched it. There are no plans for more feeders.)

Wood floors and ceilings set the outdoorsy tone the couple wanted. Red oak flooring unifies the interior, while different ceiling heights and treatments delineate areas by function. "The owners didn't want a great room effect, with living and eating in one," explains Hughes. Instead, the kitchen, dining, and living rooms are close by, side by side. Because there is an upper level, ceilings are predominately flat, says Lawton. To break up the line, he incorporated tray ceilings (also called recessed or inverted ceilings) in the living and dining rooms. The increased volume enhances the view, while striking color variations in the poplar wood ceiling encourage visitors to look up as well as out. "Poplar doesn't get used a whole lot," comments Lawton, "but it has a lot of character. The natural light and dark are very expressive." A white coffered ceiling sets off the kitchen. With an island angled to face both the living room and the dining area, this is the heart of the cabin. The brick corner hearth is a nod to Colonial Williamsburg—"my favorite place to be since college," says Phyllis.

Center-opening sliding glass doors between the dining room and covered dining porch blur the lines between outside and in. To continue the flow, the porch has the same poplar ceiling as the dining room, with two skylights to pull light into the dining room. Natural Tennessee fieldstone anchors the porch in its rustic setting.

Two upper-level bedrooms accommodate visiting family and friends. The couple's daughters—Holly lives in Orlando and Lauren in Cleveland—visit whenever possible. Phyllis's relatives also make the eleven-hour drive from Cleveland to visit the "halfbacks" (native northerners who intended to retire to Florida but opt for mid-South locations like the Carolinas).

"THERE'S NOTHING WE WOULD CHANGE, OR WISH WE DID THIS OR THAT."

The Malcolms' hilltop aerie is a bright, breezy retreat that embraces North Carolina's outdoors.

AN ACTIVE LIFE

Guests often join in the Malcolms' favorite activities of hiking, paddling, and pedaling. There's whitewater rafting in the Nantahala Gorge and canoeing on the French Broad River. Bill thrives on thirty- to fifty-mile rides with cycling buddy Tom Lawton.

When the Malcolms are not exploring the countryside, this civic-minded couple volunteers at the Swannanoa Valley Christian Ministry in Black Mountain. They also take an active role in the Creston Property Owners Association.

Both are keen gardeners. From the kitchen window, the Malcolms can admire the intricate fairy garden they created out of plants and rocks. There are wee fairies, of course, and tiny cottages. "I think up here people believe in fairies and folklore," says Phyllis. "It's mountain tradition."

Certainly, there was a happy ending for this fairy-tale cabin. The recession may have temporarily derailed the Malcolms' plans, but the three-year delay is "part of why we're so happy with the house," says Bill. "We looked at the plans for a good couple of years." During that hiatus, architect and client continued to swap ideas, move walls on paper, and generally analyze every corner.

"There's nothing we would change, or wish we did this or that," Bill states.

"We love our house," agrees Phyllis. ■

A Vermont summer house is rebuilt so that it retains old-camp charm while offering modern conveniences.

**"WE VERY MUCH WANTED
TO PRESERVE THE ORIGINAL
COTTAGE."**

BLENDING VINTAGE AND NEW

As local folks drive west on a summer's day along Vermont's Lake Fairlee, the gables of a vintage camp house come into view. Although the road is paved now, the view is much the same as it appeared on a picture postcard from 1918. The same broad porch overlooks the lake, and the chimney still pokes from the center of the roofline.

However, the house that stands now on the pristine bank is actually a clever reproduction. "The comment we get most often is, 'It looks like it's always been there,'" says Tom Porter of G.R. Porter & Sons Custom Builders. Porter was part of the team that built the "new old" home.

THE OLD CAMP

Owners John and Jeanette Freeman live on the West Coast during most of the year. They found this idyllic spot while searching for a summer home in Vermont. John knew the area because he grew up fifteen miles away in Norwich, where Porter is based. When they bought the place in 2002, people had been summering there for almost a century. Guests knew it as the Betty-Anne Inn.

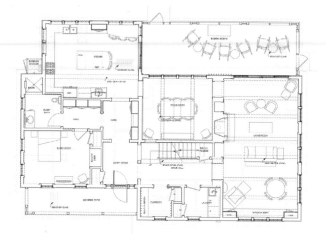

The new home sits on the old footprint but has been enlarged by 20 percent.

Green is a traditional color for camp architecture.

In the 1930s, a bed could be had for $1.25 per night, including breakfast and lunch. With views of Lake Fairlee's boating scene, the inn was a popular destination. The Freemans loved the old architectural details. Yet for every charming feature, there seemed to be an equally vexing complication. "It was built as a seasonal camp," explains architect Pi Smith, principal at Smith & Vansant Architects (SVA). "So there was no foundation. Instead of a slab, the framing of the house was built onto wooden piers and posts. The exterior was just clapboards on a wooden frame." Many of the floors were severely warped, and the place had never been winterized.

Still, the couple wrestled with plans to renovate. "Having grown up in a house built in 1812 myself, we very much wanted to preserve the original cottage," John recalls.

NATURE DECIDES

Then, Mother Nature made their decision easier. A storm in August of 2007 toppled three big pines, one of which broke right over the house. The roof and the ridge beam were badly damaged.

"We're biased toward being preservationists," says Porter. "But the house had significant structural problems." A renovation would be cost prohibitive. In addition to its structural issues, the house had ancient electrical wiring and old plumbing.

"After assessing the situation with Smith & Vansant and the Porters, we realized that it was not possible to fulfill our family's need with a simple renovation," says John. "So we decided to focus on preserving the spirit of the old house while giving ourselves the needed improvements."

RECREATING VINTAGE APPEAL

A new plan was born, one which would fool onlookers into thinking the old place had merely

The new cottage has 600 square feet of outdoor living space, including this porch, which is very similar to the one on the original home.

The upstairs bunkroom makes efficient use of space, with built-ins under the roofline.

been refurbished. The new home would sit on the old footprint, yet be enlarged by 20 percent.

With a great deal of planning and plenty of documentation, the character of the old place was recaptured. "We used the same roof pitches, the same gable," explains Smith. "We took pains to recover details, such as the eave returns." The new porch features a pair of replica columns, with latticework between them. New window groupings are similar to the old, and the chimney rises in the same location. "So many people have said, 'We're glad you fixed it up,'" SVA's project manager Jason Gaddis notes with a grin.

The kitchen was moved to the lake side of the house for the expansive views.

The look and feel inside the new summer home is in keeping with the paneled aesthetic of the traditional camp it replaced.

The new fireplace was built with stones from a nearby quarry, and the mantel was made from wood salvaged from an old Vermont fly-fishing rod factory.

ADDING MODERN COMFORTS

Starting from scratch allowed the architects to design a more modern layout than would have been possible in a renovation. "The old floor plan was squirrelly," adds Smith. "And the sequence of entering the house had not been well thought out." The new version provides for a mudroom, and the location of the staircase was adjusted to save space.

The living room was recreated almost exactly, down to the cased wooden beams and the window pattern. But instead of facing the road, the new kitchen has sweeping views of the lake.

The new home pays homage to the paneled, traditional camp it replaced. Yet all the exposed wood and painted beams can make a house appear dark. So the new design includes a subtle lift of the ceiling height in the kitchen and on the porch. Fixed transom windows added over several interior doors pull more daylight into the rooms.

The bunkroom upstairs was rebuilt for the two Freeman children plus two guests. Each bedroom has new built-ins under the steepest parts of the roofline, "utilizing space that was wasted before," Smith explains.

EVERYTHING OLD IS NEW AGAIN

In keeping with the antique aesthetic, original architectural elements were repurposed. For instance, the upstairs hallway features seven old doors from the previous structure; Smith repeated the five-paneled theme in the new millwork downstairs.

Another feature worth saving was the beautiful clear Douglas fir flooring found in part of the camp's main level. But there weren't enough floorboards in decent condition. So the Freemans hunted for salvaged fir boards, which proved elusive. "Until I found them on Craigslist in San Diego," John remembers. "A salvager had taken down an old Michigan distillery from the 1880s, and a lot of board feet were available." He had an entire train carload shipped to Porter's millwork shop. That fir became flooring and wainscoting for the main level, as well as a top for the kitchen island and an eating bar.

Upstairs, the fir transitions to pine. Remember those trees that fell on the house? Porter milled them into flooring and wainscoting for the second level.

CHARM THAT'S ACCESSIBLE TO ALL

The Freemans needed to make the house accessible to a wheelchair-bound family member. (Since John is a Vermont native, he knew that many Lake Fairlee homes "were up and down a number of stairs. We actually bought this place sight unseen because of its level property.") And the Freeman family didn't want just a single accessible door; they wanted every door to be accessible.

With a fresh design, the accessibility needs of the house became simpler to address. Smith had recently dealt with many of the same issues in her own home. "My father has mobility issues, and I had to deal with finding graceful ways of getting him in and out of my house." She was determined to execute a design which did not smack of bulky wheelchair ramps.

The result is so subtle that visitors to the house will not likely notice its accessibility. "The frame was actually sunk into the new concrete foundation," not built on top of it. "We lowered the whole house down as close to grade as we could," Smith says. A visitor with a wheelchair can roll right into any of the doors, around the kitchen island, and out onto the dock. The downstairs shower has a roll-in design. And the eating bar in the kitchen is comfortable at wheelchair height. Controls for the stove's vent fan and light are on switches on the backsplash.

COLORING BETWEEN THE LINES

Now came the fun part: color. "My wife is a graphic designer, and great with color," John says. "What are there, thirty-three different paint colors in the house?"

"Not that many," his wife insists. With the assistance of designer Denise Welch-May of DPF Design in nearby White River Junction, Jeanette chose an appealing palate reminiscent of the old inn.

"SO MANY PEOPLE HAVE SAID, 'WE'RE GLAD YOU FIXED IT UP.'"

The cottage owners and their architect did such a good job of retaining the character of the old camp house that passersby think the old place has merely been renovated.

In the kitchen, living room, and hallways, shades of green contrast nicely with warm wood tones. "The green downstairs, along with the fir wainscoting, has the same look and feel that you can still see in the older camp buildings," Smith says. And while green is a traditional camp house choice, the Betty-Anne Inn boasted brightly colored rooms. The bedrooms had furniture painted in a distinctive color, as well. The new design calls for each bedroom to have a different hue on the floor; there is a red bedroom set off with yellow window trim, as well as an orange room and a blue one. "I generally like white," says Jeanette, "but it just doesn't feel right in Vermont."

As with most home design projects, there was some compromise between husband and wife. "He liked the unpainted wood," recalls Welch-May, "and Jeanette wanted more color." In the final design, both were important. "We trimmed the fir wainscoting with painted wood," or set a painted window frame into a paneled wall.

The result is a beautiful, thoughtful vacation home. While the Freemans currently spend winters in California, they did build a year-round cabin, so a Vermont winter wonderland awaits them. "Now we have a fantastic house for all seasons," says John Freeman, "even if it took a falling tree to get us going." ∎

Because the Hinchey home is nestled in the trees, it affords great peeks at beautiful vignettes from its back porch, which overlooks the lake from a steep perch.

"WE KNEW WE BOTH WANTED A LOG HOME, THOUGH FOR DIFFERENT REASONS."

THE WAITING GAME

As the fourth largest state in the U.S., Montana draws land-seekers from all over the country. After all, the "Last Best Place" abounds with miles of wilderness and pristine property for sale. Yet, surprisingly, when Montana residents Julianne and Sean Hinchey set out to purchase a lot for their weekend retreat, they had to wait several years for their dream site to materialize.

"We had our hearts set on Lake Five," explains Julianne, describing a tranquil community in the foothills of Glacier National Park. "Unfortunately, there are only about thirty cabins or so on the lake, and it's really hard to come by property there since most people have had the land in their families for years."

Though nothing surfaced initially, Julianne and Sean didn't give up. They had fallen head-over-heels in love with the area—and with each other—during their law school years, when they often visited Sean's family, who had a place nearby along the Flathead River.

The couple wrote to every landowner on Lake Five, requesting that they be notified should anyone wish to sell.

What could be dreamier than waking up to the sounds of nature and your very own lakefront view?

Costs for building on a steep lot can quickly escalate. A narrow footprint can help—less material will be needed—while still providing great views.

Though it didn't happen overnight, the Hincheys eventually received a call. They jumped at the opportunity to own a picturesque lot with about 200 feet of lake frontage. The couple opted to keep a trailer on the site for a few years while they planned their dream cabin.

"We knew we both wanted a log home, though for different reasons," says Julianne. "I grew up in Anchorage, Alaska, and my family had a weekend lakeside home that I loved. My husband is from California, and he was just psyched about the whole rugged log home thing."

LAYING THE LOGS

Thankfully, getting the log home project started proved a lot easier than finding the property. After studying a number of log home magazines, the Hincheys brainstormed a basic floor plan, then brought it to Top Notch Log Homes in nearby Columbia Falls, Montana. (The company has since renamed itself Natural Log Creations.)

IN TOO STEEP

The biggest challenge was the steepness of the lot and the fact that the Hincheys wanted to build their cabin just twenty-five feet from the lake. They acquired a variance to do so fairly easily, however. Then the staff at Top Notch created a plan for building the home into the hill.

"We were able to squeeze the home in between the trees and the view, so the area where the cabin sits is incredibly cozy and well protected," says Julianne.

"Basically, we wanted a place where we'd be able to just look out on the lake and unwind," shares Julianne. "So we needed a floor plan that would maximize the views without taking away too many of the trees on the site."

Aiding in the aged
appearance of the cabin
is the use of vintage
furnishings. Why buy new
when you can reuse?

Visitors to the Hinchey home all agree that the lake and mountain views are simply breathtaking.

The sleeping loft feels almost like a tree house.

Handsome fir cabinetry is offset by striking slate countertops and a kitchen island topped with a copper overlay. The large logs overhead add a dramatic note.

The log package is just as striking as the view itself. The custom, handcrafted log home features hand-scribed tamarack logs with fully scribed natural corners. All of the logs were hand-selected and hand-peeled, and scribed with single-notch, full-round corners," says Kevin Peterson, owner of Top Notch Log Homes. "All of the logs are dry, standing-dead timber from Montana, ranging in size from fourteen to twenty inches."

The crew at Top Notch took several months to build the custom package on the company lot. Then it was shipped to the Hincheys' site, where the team erected the log shell within two weeks. "The building process went very smoothly," recalls the log provider.

Once the Top Notch crew was done with its portion of the job, the Hincheys needed a master builder to complete the 1,500-square-foot retreat. They found that in local carpenter Bruce Jungnitsch.

LIVING THE LIFE

Thanks to his fine craftsmanship, the Hincheys' cabin boasts exquisite detail and is a lasting tribute to the man who built it. The home's old-fashioned décor, combined with its breathtaking views and come-on-in ambiance, lends an irresistible charm. Comfy leather sofas in the living room invite cabingoers to kick back and enjoy views of both the fireplace and the majestic lake. "It's exactly what we envisioned and more," says Julianne.

WHAT'S OLD IS NEW

The home's decorating style complements its traditional log look. "We wanted to make it feel like an old-style log lodge but on a smaller scale," she explains. "Its old-fashioned chinking, divided windows, and other details make it feel like one of the old lodges in Glacier Park, as if it has been here for a hundred years." Given a special finish, new fir flooring took on a patina of age. Fir cabinetry in the kitchen is offset by slate counter-tops and an island topped with a copper overlay.

Family pieces, such as a 1960s solid wood dining room set that belonged to Julianne's mother, and the great room tables made by Julianne's grandfather from monkey pod wood (a tropical hardwood native to Hawaii), lend a vintage look. Old and new come together in the master bath, where traditional log chinking vies for attention with the eye-catching shower tiles. A gray slate floor adds additional texture. The roomy apron tub was a must-have for Julianne.

Whether they are hiking, fishing, or simply sitting on the deck, the Hincheys know they have created a place where they can always unwind. They love spending Christmas there together. "It's just so quiet because no one else is around, and it seems like we have the whole lake to ourselves," says Julianne. "It's like having a great big yard for hockey, skating, and more."

"IT'S JUST SO QUIET BECAUSE NO ONE ELSE IS AROUND, AND IT
SEEMS LIKE WE HAVE THE WHOLE LAKE TO OURSELVES."

From the living room you can sit back and enjoy the views of both the fireplace and the majestic lake.

Old and new come together in the master bath, where traditional log chinking vies for attention with the eye-catching shower tiles.

"As lawyers, we lead somewhat of a hectic life, and our cabin provides great solitude and relaxation for us," she explains. "When we arrive, our shoulders immediately go down and we feel much better. When we walk out on that deck and take in the view, it's like being in heaven."

As the Hincheys sit and gaze across Lake Five, they can't help but think about their quest to find land, the fine craftsmanship of the late Bruce Jungnitsch, and the great memories they have created at their weekend retreat. Julianne sums it up best, saying, "It really is a dream come true." ■

> "I CARRIED AROUND A TATTERED PHOTOGRAPH IN MY WALLET OF MY DREAM CABIN."

A BOYHOOD DREAM COMES TRUE

As a boy growing up in Boulder, Colorado, Ted Valentiner aspired to one day own a little log cabin in the woods. "I had a picture in my head of what it would look like," says Ted. "I even carried around a tattered photograph in my wallet of my dream cabin."

Several decades later, the dream became reality. In 2012, Ted and his wife, Linda Shannon-Valentiner, purchased a lake property in Whitefish, Montana. Nestled in the foothills of the Rockies near Glacier National Park, this location had it all: an extensive network of trails for riding their horses, Buzz and Whiskey Pete; trout fishing for Ted on Whitefish Lake; and for Linda, lots of nearby vintage festivals and fairs—her passion.

A HOME MADE OF HISTORY

The couple envisioned a year-round retreat that reflected their laid-back western lifestyle. They also wanted the cabin to blend in seamlessly with its surroundings. Montana Log Homes (MLH) in Kalispell was tapped as builder. Meeting with Eric Bachofner, the firm's co-owner and draftsman,

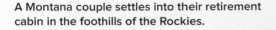

A Montana couple settles into their retirement cabin in the foothills of the Rockies.

The front porch of the owners' log home near Glacier National Park.

The ladder leads to a sleeping nook above the kitchen.

the first thing Ted and Linda said was that they wanted their new cabin to appear old. Accordingly, they chose a style of construction that features square timbers with hand-crafted dovetail joinery at the corners. "The whole philosophy of the dovetail construction is to make a structure look much older than it is," explains MLH's co-owner, Brad Neu. Using standing dead lodgepole pine logs from the Northwest makes the cabin look as if it's been around since the 1800s. Gaps between the timbers are filled with chinking material. (Note: Much of today's chinking is an elastromeric material that's flexible, moving with logs as they shift and settle.)

Construction got under way in June. A highlight of the process was seeing their cabin arrive on a flatbed truck and go up in a single day. "We sat in lawn chairs on the mountainside and watched them stack the logs like Lincoln Logs," marvels Ted.

DESIGNING WITH BALANCE

When designing the cabin, items topping Linda's wish list were a large, inviting living room and a luxurious master bathroom. But the couple wanted to keep the size of the home to a minimum. Bachofner knew that meant that the kitchen would have to be small and practical, yet still warm and inviting. "The end result is a cozy cabin look on the outside with a classy great-room feel as you step inside," says Bachofner. "It's a combination that is seldom achieved."

The metal on the front of the kitchen counter was salvaged from an old barn. The stools were a gift from a friend who sells vintage goods at a local vintage store.

The cabin is bursting with vintage furnishings and appliances, like this stove.

This is the interior of the one-room cabin on the owners' property that was modeled after a trapper's cabin.

LAYOUT AND DESIGN

The 2,160-square-foot cabin comprises two levels. The main floor (1,080 square feet) features a spacious living room and a master suite with French doors that open to a porch. A generous ensuite bathroom boasts a fireplace, claw-foot tub, and four-foot-long, wall-mounted sink. The glass shower has a pebble floor and wall tile that resembles reclaimed barnwood.

Above the kitchen is a sleeping nook accessible by ladder. The area was originally designed to be closed off and used for storage, but Linda wanted to optimize sleeping quarters. "Once we have grandchildren, that extra bed will come in handy," says Linda. "Right now, the odd nap gets taken up there."

Because of the cabin's small footprint, it was important to use space efficiently. So instead of closing off the upper walls with drywall, they asked their builder for cupboards reaching to the ceiling. This space above closets and laundry could store seasonal items and unsightly electrical wires.

The original design didn't call for a walk-out basement. But the Valentiners realized after excavation that because the site is on a hillside, they could double their square footage and create a guest suite large enough for a bed, bath, office, and kitchenette. "It's designed like a studio/old-fashioned hotel room," says Linda.

"THESE BUILDINGS ALL HAVE A HERITAGE, AND WE WANTED TO PRESERVE, HONOR, AND MAINTAIN THAT HERITAGE."

The garage also has a studio feel—with a sleeping area, workout room, and fireplace—and acts as the couple's "creation space." Linda uses it as a sewing area, and Ted makes leather goods like belts and saddles.

CELEBRATING HERITAGE

Since the couple is interested in preserving the historical integrity of Montana's structures, they incorporated reclaimed lumber with a rich history. For instance, the planks in the two-toned front door came from a hundred-year-old Montana schoolhouse. The thick butcher-block kitchen counter was once part of a 1940s General Mills grain elevator, also from Montana. "These buildings all have a heritage, and we wanted to preserve, honor, and maintain that heritage," says Ted. The cabin's floors, ceilings, and the top bit of the chimney breast (the area above the mantle) were crafted from reclaimed barnwood. The bottom portion of the chimney is made from local stone.

The master bathroom includes a fireplace, shower (left foreground), and tub.

The French doors of the master bedroom open to a porch that provides the perfect spot to enjoy a Montana sunset with a glass of wine.

FUNKY MIX OF DÉCOR

Linda also selected the faucets, fixtures, windows, and plumbing. "Putting it all together is my passion," she explains. Because Linda is a repurposing mastermind, the cabin is bursting with vintage furnishings. She fashioned the chaise longue in the master bathroom from an old handcart. She also converted an antique coffee grinder into part of a bedroom lamp.

The chandelier in the living room was made by neighbor Bobby Giles, who fashioned it from an oak barrel topped by a saw blade from an old mill.

In a downstairs bedroom are a sofa and velvet chair that once belonged to famous entertainer Rudy Vallée. "They're in mint condition because Rudy put them in storage in the 1920s, where they remained until we purchased them," says Ted.

Linda adores retro fashion décor, so throughout the cabin she has positioned several head-and-torso mannequins. "Mixing the rustic French look with American West style is another passion of mine," she says.

CHRISTMAS SURPRISE

Since Ted was working overseas during much of the cabin's construction, Linda took daily pictures to show the progress. She purposely neglected to photograph one piece of the project, however. Linda had asked her brother Tony to build a special Christmas surprise for her husband: a one-room cabin located a hundred yards downhill from the main cabin.

When Linda first took Ted to see his surprise, it was like a scene from a movie. Snow fell from the night sky at a fierce clip as the couple maneuvered their car through blowing snowdrifts. Then, Ted laid awestruck eyes on his trapper's cabin. "It was lit up and looked exactly like the photo I'd been carrying for years," recalls Ted. "I couldn't believe how perfectly Linda had captured my vision."

Ted and Linda chose furnishings and finishes—including holiday decorations—that spoke to their laid-back western lifestyle.

PLAYTIME

Now that Ted is retired, the couple looks forward to just enjoying their new surroundings. "Earning a living and building our home has been all-consuming for the past two years," says Linda. "We can't wait to get involved with whatever comes our way. There's no shortage of options."

That includes fishing, horseback riding, canoeing, snowshoeing, and cross-country skiing. "We live next to a Nordic Center with a beautiful trail that goes around the lake," says Linda. "It's quite a workout!" They also enjoy hosting luncheons, dinners, and holiday celebrations for friends, neighbors, and family. Gatherings will no doubt increase now that they are settled in and living the dream. ■

THE OUTDOORSY CABIN

So much of cabin living revolves around connecting with nature. In this section, you'll find cabins with fabulous outdoor living spaces, including porches, decks, patios, and breezeways. Such spaces expand a cabin's livable area during good weather, and when they're well designed, the boundary between indoors and outdoors is seamless. There's an added surprise in this section: a cabin that's not beside a lake but actually floating *on* the lake!

One family builds their dream lake cabin with an 1800s barn

BARNWOOD BEAUTY

The annual pilgrimage started back in 1947, when Iowan Charles Van Werden first heard the call of Leech Lake in the Minnesota Northwoods. A mecca for anglers, the pristine waters teem with walleye, perch, northern pike, and the elusive muskie.

After Charles and his wife had children, Mrs. Van Werden insisted he take the family—rather than his fishing chums—to the lake. Every summer, they bunked at Carlson Resort, run by Swedish immigrants Auggie and Mettie Carlson. Over the years, new generations followed in their footsteps. Despite being spread across different states, for two weeks every summer much of the clan gathered at the rustic resort.

In 1975, three of Charles's grown children bought the property after the Carlsons retired. By the time the fourth generation came along a few decades later, several family members had purchased adjacent cabins. "Camp," as they call it, was beginning to feel mighty cramped. So when a run-down cabin directly north of Carlson's went on the market, Charles's granddaughter Jane Lorentzen and her husband, John, pounced on it. The Des Moines, Iowa, couple spent the next two years researching architectural styles. "We wanted

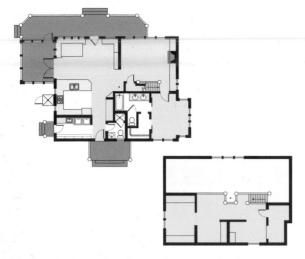

The simple floor plan places the master bedroom and two bathrooms on the main floor with two more bedrooms in the loft.

In the master bathroom, there's a combination of painted and unpainted wood.

to build a nice new place that looked old," says Jane.

Each Lorentzen family member got to choose one element of the design. Jane chose reclaimed wood. John, a screened porch. Daughter Maddie wanted a loft. Son Will, twelve at the time, requested a fire pole. The couple interviewed several architects, all of whom scoffed at this last notion. All except Jeff and Matt Balmer, that is. The brothers own Lands End Development, a design-build firm based in Crosslake, Minnesota. "Cool!" was the Balmers' response. "That sealed the deal," Jane recalls.

A WOODEN PUZZLE

Back in Iowa, Jane's dad knew of an old post and beam barn that the owner wanted torn down. If the Lorentzens removed the barn, promised its owner, they could have the wood. Jeff flew in to inspect the timber, thrilled to unearth old-growth pine preserved by mounds of hay.

The Lorentzens had the barn dismantled; every plank, beam, and artifact was trucked to the lake. Once unloaded, the Balmers sorted through the material like so many puzzle pieces. Floors, ceilings, trim, built-ins—ultimately, every last bit of the barn was repurposed, down to an ice hook that hangs from a peg on the fireplace mantle.

SIMPLE PLAN

The reclaimed wood's varied textures and colors create a rustic, casual vibe. "The owners insisted on building a cabin that could be put through its paces," says Jeff. "Dirty dogs, wet kids, sandy floors— it's all okay." The cabin is a favorite gathering spot for extended family. "We might not see each other all year long, but two weeks every summer, all thirteen cousins convene here," says Jane.

The owners' twelve-year-old
requested a fire pole.

The kitchen's cabinets contrast nicely with the hood over the range, which came from the barn's corrugated metal roof.

The simple floor plan features a living room with a massive lake stone fireplace and an adjoining dining area. A trestle table crafted from barnwood seats eight—twelve, if small children are present. At the rear of the cabin are a kitchen (the range hood is fashioned from the barn's corrugated metal roof), a powder room, and a master bedroom suite.

The owners also incorporated a mudroom complete with sink, washer/dryer, and lots of storage. An outdoor shower minimizes the amount of sand tracked inside. (The family named the cabin "Sandy Sheets" in honor of Jane's childhood at camp. Despite valiant efforts to rinse her feet, she inevitably found grains in her bed every night. "It drove me nuts at the time," she admits. "But now it's a great cabin memory.")

Jane's grandfather, Charles Van Werden, catching a muskie (circa 1940s).

Quite often, the porch is the most commonly used room in a cabin.

"DIRTY DOGS, WET KIDS, SANDY FLOORS—IT'S ALL OKAY."

Upstairs, a sleeping loft boasts two sets of built-in pine bunk beds. Another cozy slumber spot has a built-in double bed with a trundle. These areas are not closed off with doors, but rather separated by a curtain. "The cabins I grew up in were just like this, and I loved it," says Jane.

GAMES AND FISHING

In the living room, a small table with an ongoing jigsaw puzzle beckons to anyone passing by. Other cherished pastimes include cooking, reading, and sitting round the campfire devouring s'mores. "My favorite thing is to sip a glass of wine and watch the sunset," says Jane. "It's also fun to sit on the screen porch and watch storms blow in. The 'pingy' sound of the rain on the corrugated metal roof is soothing." (After a storm, crawdads scurry on the beach; the kids collect the small freshwater lobsters for an old-fashioned boil.)

For the Lorentzens, it's all about the lake.

When the weather's nice, the family gravitates to the water. Sailing, skiing, wakeboarding, tubing, jumping from the water trampoline—"it's all about the lake," declares John.

In the heart of summer, the Lorentzens boat to Bear Island, anchoring on the soft sugar-sand beach. The kids play catch with Burdie, the family's two-year-old golden retriever, while the adults unload a picnic lunch.

The family also holds a fish fry every summer. The tradition started decades earlier when Auggie introduced Jane, her brothers, and their cousins to fishing with long cane poles. "He was very patient, even when we got hooked in the head with fishhooks," she recalls. "When we came back later, our parents met us in the harbor with their Super 8 cameras to film us with our loot."

PARTY ON!

These days, new traditions are forged year-round at the cabin. John enjoys duck and grouse hunting in the fall. Winter promises ice fishing and miles of exercise on cross-country ski trails. Some years, the Lorentzens attend the International Eelpout Festival held in February in nearby Walker, Minnesota. Named for one of the ugliest bottom-dwelling fish, the festival is like a "frozen Mardi Gras," says Jane.

Of course, every day at the lake is a celebration. Jane still recalls that first morning in the new cabin. She was making breakfast when the pitter-patter of feet came from the loft. The click of the gate unlatching was followed by the sound of little campers sliding down the brass fire pole. "When their feet hit the floor, the party had begun," says Jane. "We have a love for this place that's hard to describe." ■

The floor of the cabin comes from the Iowa barn's exterior. The fireplace is made of the lake's stone, and the mantel is fashioned from a barn beam, as is the dining room trestle table.

The use of low-profile decks, as well as a weathered gray-green cedar lap sliding, help this retreat blend into the landscape.

"YOU DON'T WANT YOUR
SECOND HOME TO LOOK LIKE
YOUR FIRST HOME."

SUMMER CAMP REVISITED

Imagine all the fun of summer camp, only with comfy beds and decent bathrooms. That's the vision one family had for their vacation home on Norris Lake near the Smoky Mountains of Tennessee. The cabin's design, by Daryl Johnson of Johnson Architecture in Knoxville, partners with the land's natural beauty to recreate a grown-up version of the traditional camp experience.

"I was excited about the project, and that radiated back to the client," Johnson says. "It took us out of the realm of our normal design process and let us play."

FUN AT CAMP

Johnson incorporated iconic memories of summer camp and civilized them with modern conveniences. Remember sauntering along a nature path from your cabin to the dining hall? Johnson reinvented that walk by separating the bedroom blocks from the main living areas and then connecting them with a covered dogtrot. So, "campers" can experience the outdoors upon leaving the "bunkhouse," yet still be protected from the weather.

If you want to avoid redecorating every few years, choose classic patterns in soft, warm colors.

Area rugs are a great addition to a cabin where you know the kids or grandkids will be playing on the floor.

There are touches of whimsy, too. Johnson built a roofed tree house that matches the cabin's exterior and connected it to the bedroom block by a swinging rope bridge about twenty-five feet long. Older children can spend the night there but still have easy access to the main house and bathrooms.

And a scenic overlook deck above the dogtrot, high enough for a panoramic view of Norris Lake, has a fire pole for a quick, exciting ride back down. Now what camper, young or old, wouldn't like that?

LODGE FEEL

The main living space channels a camp lodge vibe with its large stone fireplace and open-rafter ceiling. No load-bearing walls block the views from one side to the other. Instead, handhewn Douglas fir timbers rise twelve feet to the center ridgeline, supporting the ceiling and dividing the living and dining rooms visually.

The main living area is separated from the sleeping quarters by an outdoor covered dogtrot. Walking outside to get to a bedroom provides the feeling of walking to the summer camp "bunkhouse."

The oval shape of braided rugs softens a room, and the colors and texture will make any space feel cozy.

When decorating your retreat, don't restrain yourself. Try something different, like using different baskets, barrels, or buckets.

The owners wanted windows hinged at the top that could be opened outward by a pulley and a rope.

The ceiling slopes down gently to about eight feet tall around the outer edge. All perimeter walls are light or whitewashed shiplap wood with flush joints; floors are polished heart pine.

Ninety-degree brackets on the exterior walls are part of the window system that became a key element of the design. The owners wanted windows hinged at the top that could be opened outward by a pulley and a rope. The brackets serve as a fulcrum for the pulley. Ropes inside are pulled to open the windows out. When fully open, they extend at a ninety-degree angle parallel to the deck to open up the cabin completely.

Because the windows hinge at the top, they may be opened partially in the rain to bring in fresh air. "Every room has them," Johnson says of the custom-made windows. Of course, the open windows needed screens—a complicating factor, but a design challenge that Johnson embraced. "We couldn't get any window manufacturer to make them for us, so we had to figure out a way to do it," he says. Johnson also added a large screened porch off the dining area that allows the owners and their guests to enjoy the outdoor air without mosquitoes.

BLENDING IN

The retreat sits high on a bluff overlooking Norris Lake. However, the owners did not want to call attention to the house and interrupt the natural view one would have upon looking up from the lake. Rather than stone, the owners chose a weathered gray-green horizontal cedar lap siding.

"We didn't want the home to stick up out of the rock," Johnson comments. "The owners wanted it to feel like it had grown out of the hillside." Johnson designed a meandering driveway that opens to the vacation home site. At the end of the drive, the place reveals itself, low and almost hovering over the ground.

Johnson is keen on melding his designs with nature. His use of low-profile decks on this retreat, no more than a foot or two off the soil, helps blend it into the landscape. The roof has a modest pitch with extra-wide overhangs that do away with the need for gutters and downspouts. Rain chains and catch basins are utilized at certain points around the structure.

VACATION LIVING

Kreis Beall of Blackberry Farm Design in Walland, Tennessee, lent her expertise to the interior design. The renowned furniture market in High Point, North Carolina, was close enough for a trip, and Beall accompanied the homeowners to check out the possibilities. They chose hickory furniture and rough textures in contrast to the family's

The owners chose hickory furniture and rough textures for a more relaxed atmosphere.

"YOU DO WANT YOUR GUESTS TO FEEL LIKE FAMILY."

year-round home. "You don't want your second home to look like your first home," Beall says. "You want it to live the way you live on vacation."

Hooks occasionally take the place of closets. Heavily grained hickory tops the breakfast-bar island in the kitchen, and the countertops along the walls are heart pine. To add color to the rooms awash in sunlight, Beall layered in quilts collected by the homeowners, braided rugs to tie in the colors, and deeply textured fabrics. The cabin was built several years ago, yet the décor remains timeless. Beall shied away from trendy design features and deliberately chose classic patterns and soft, warm colors that would not need periodic updating.

Beall balanced style with comfort and focused on low-maintenance living that wouldn't be rattled by kids and dogs. "You don't want your family to feel like guests," Beall says. "And you do want your guests to feel like family." ■

The cabin has an open-rafter ceiling and no interior walls from one end to the other. Twelve-foot hand-hewn Douglas fir timbers compose a center spine that divides the space.

This Tennessee cabin is truly on the water.

FLOATING CABIN

While cabins can be situated in the woods or the mountains, for many people the quintessential cabin is located on the water.

Unlike most folks, though, Rich and Marla Thomas interpret "on the water" literally. *Their oasis actually floats.* Every window offers stellar lake views, and the water's edge is just a few steps right out the door. Its wraparound deck doubles as a dock; along with the requisite outdoor furniture are mooring cleats and a water slide for daughter Katelyn.

The Thomases belong to a unique floating community at Stardust Marina and Resort on Norris Lake, Tennessee.

PERSONAL TOUCHES

"Originally, the house was built on the shore near the marina, filled with furniture, and then pushed out to the current site," explains Rich. When purchased, the floating house had an "ocean beach" feel. Now, cedar siding and faux rock on the front columns give the exterior a "lake house" look. One of Marla's water-skis, hand-painted with the motto "Life Is Better at the Lake," hangs over the front door. Accents like Marla's childhood skis and Rich's fishing rods and lures add a personal touch. The coffee table is a U.S. Marine Corps

Plenty of color amps up the Thomases' retreat summertime factor.

The balcony off the master bedroom is the best place to watch the sun rise over the lake.

footlocker that belonged to Marla's dad. "It's a nice way to keep his memory alive at a place we know he would enjoy," says Marla. Making the cabin feel like their own, though, was no easy feat. "For our renovations, everything we needed had to be brought over by boat," Rich notes. (While the Thomases are able to tote groceries and nominal supplies in their boats, Stardust rents pontoons for larger cargo.)

LET'S GO

Though Norris Lake is a seven-hour drive from home, Rich and Marla make the trip every chance they get.

"We're both retired schoolteachers," says Marla. "Although we bought the floating house two years before retirement, we are still on a school schedule due to Katelyn." The family spends the entire summer, as well as school breaks, at the lake. Once parked at the marina, the family hops aboard one of their two moored boats to reach the cabin. To fully enjoy the lake, their "fleet" also includes a personal watercraft, a paddleboat, and two kayaks. Boats and toys are docked on all sides of the floating house, then stowed away during the off-season.)

NEVER DULL

What's the best part of living on the water? "Everything!" chorus the Thomases. Chiefly, the ability to indulge in water activities on the spur of the moment. Then there's watching the sun rise over the lake, viewed from the deck off the master bedroom. (This balcony gets the nod as best design feature.) With no grass to mow or property to tend, the Thomases find life on their private "island" extremely relaxing.

Deciding what to do each day is the hardest part. They keep busy swimming, waterskiing,

The red leather sofa provides a pop of color in the open floor plan design.

and fishing for striper and smallmouth and largemouth bass. Kneeboarding, tubing, paddleboarding, and kayaking are also favorite pastimes. "We love to be outdoors as a family and encourage our friends and family to join in on the fun," says Rich. "Striper fishing is an adventure all on its own because the sheer strength and size of a big striper can intimidate even a veteran angler. Watching a new fisherman or child struggle to reel a huge fish in—while screaming with excitement —is priceless. The same can be said for those who are able to ski, kneeboard, or wakeboard for the first time. It's very rewarding for us as well as them."

This was especially true when Katelyn learned to water-ski. "It was truly memorable," recalls Marla. "The further out of the water she got, the more her facial expression showed delight and excitement! We were so proud of her for making it on the first attempt."

For renovations, everything had to be brought over by boat.

Life jackets are a must for all water activities—even for the family pet.

(Another learning experience was not as delightful: Two cell phones were lost in a week that first summer on the water. "We now have a waterproof iPhone with a life jacket," says Rich.)

Life jackets are a must for water safety, even for the family's Maltese-Yorkie dog named Rosebud. "The ducks and geese visit the floating house every day," explains Marla. "Rosebud gets so excited that she often falls in while trying to greet them. She is a good swimmer but wears a life jacket for safety just like the kids." Rosebud's life jacket also comes in handy, as she's an avid boater. "She loves to ride on the front point of the kayak," says Marla. "It allows her to see everything that is going on." The Thomases installed a dock ladder so Rosebud, the kids, and Grandma can easily climb out of the water.

When they can tear themselves away from the lake, the family also enjoys hiking and caving at the Chuck Swan Wildlife Management Area, a 25,000-acre forest just across the lake. "We still have one large cave to find and explore," said Marla. "There are also numerous caves around the lake that you can explore by boating right up to them."

THE UPS AND DOWNS
OF OWNING A FLOATING CABIN

Most floating cabins are not located within catwalk slips/docks, but since they occupy space within a marina's harbor, owners still pay a mooring fee. Typically, an annual lease is needed to rent the space.

Utilities consist of waste pump-out, water, and electric. All floating cabins are required to have waste pumped out regularly. While some marinas include this in their monthly mooring charge, others charge an additional cost. For example: On average, in the Norris Lake Marina, this amounts to about $450 per season in addition to the mooring fee.

Water may be provided by the marina, and it may be included in the monthly mooring fee or billed separately monthly or annually. For floating cabins where water is not supplied by the marina, typically a lake water pump will be installed. These pumps allow the lake water to be used for sinks or showers, while residents carry in water for drinking or cooking. Another option is installing a system that treats lake water for drinking.

Additionally, electric/shore power is not available at every marina. When power is available, electricity is metered and read monthly or quarterly by either the marina or local utility company. Most marinas require the owner to purchase and maintain the shore-to-cabin power cable, which consists of underwater mining cable. If a retreat is for sale and is hooked to power and the cable is being included in the sale, the listing will usually state: "Shore Power Included."

What's the best part of living on the water? Everything!

"WE LOVE TO BE OUTDOORS AS A FAMILY AND ENCOURAGE OUR FRIENDS AND FAMILY TO JOIN IN ON THE FUN."

Of course, spending the Fourth of July at the cabin is an American tradition, and this floating retreat is no exception. "We always have a full house," says Rich. The gang enjoys watching "Fire on the Water," touted as the largest private fireworks show in Tennessee.

While the days may be full of activities, the Thomases love the evenings, too. "Ending the day with fresh grilled striper, then making s'mores on the campfire [a dish fire pit on the side deck] and rekindling the day's events is the perfect way to wind down," says Rich. ■

Porch sitting in this community is just like other neighborhoods, except the conversations are from porch to boat, not as neighbors walk by.

A Chicago couple builds a small retreat
that merges seamlessly with the outdoors
on North Carolina's Haw River.

"WE WANTED PEOPLE TO
FORGET WHETHER THEY WERE
INSIDE OR OUTSIDE."

AN OUTDOORSY LITTLE RIVER CABIN

Chicago winters can be brutal. North Carolina winters, on the other hand, are awfully nice. Several years ago, Chicagoans Jim and Kitty decided to buy a ten-acre piece of land on the Haw River in Pittsboro, twenty minutes from UNC–Chapel Hill. The plan was to someday build a retirement home on the property. Three years after purchasing the lot, however, Jim started to get antsy.

"I got to thinking that I'd like to enjoy the land while we were still young," says Jim. "I wanted to build a retreat we could start using right away."

The idea of coordinating construction from 800 miles away didn't thrill Kitty. But once the couple met with Georgia Bizios of Bizios Architect, in nearby Durham, North Carolina, both Kitty and Jim relaxed. Georgia was a competent, trustworthy, highly creative architect brimming with ideas.

The west side of the cabin features a stone wall that evokes a castle feel.

The east side deck makes that side of the home feel airy and open.

BUILDING THE GUESTHOUSE FIRST

The project was unique because zoning in the county allowed for two structures on the property: a primary home 2,500 square feet or larger, and a guesthouse that could not exceed 1,000 square feet of heated space.

Since the Delanys wanted a getaway retreat sooner rather than later, they chose to first erect a guest cabin. It consists of a main room with a cathedral ceiling, a small kitchen, two bedrooms, and two baths.

The couple walked the site with Georgia to determine where the main house and barn might eventually go. Making these plans enabled them to figure out the right spot on which to build the guest cabin.

"Due to the size restrictions, we had to get creative in our design," recalls Georgia. "We attached an additional 1,500 square feet of outdoor living space by way of a wraparound porch and decking. There is also a small outdoor sleeping loft above the screened porch."

AN INSPIRED USE OF MATERIALS

The design of the Delanys' retreat is unique in that it transitions from stone to wood to glass to screen to open air. Therefore, the perspective changes based on which part of the cabin one is facing.

"Imagine the cabin as a parallelogram," suggests Georgia. "On the west side, there are stone walls with windows. That side feels more castle-like. The living room and entryway are a bit more open with wood siding and additional windows. On the east side is the screened porch that continues out onto the deck, making that side of the home airy, perforated, and open."

Georgia says that when designing homes, she draws inspiration from the rural North Carolina vernacular—barns, tobacco houses, log cabins.

The stone of the chimney becomes the visual anchor for the whole cabin. The mantel is simple so as not to distract from the stone, and the hearth is raised for fireside seating.

This stairway leads to a small outdoor sleeping loft with a twin bed that sits above the screened porch.

She's also inspired by the temperate climate, the land's topography, and the indigenous plant material.

"We used gable metal roofs, wood siding, stone materials, a wraparound porch, and a big screened porch," notes Georgia. "These choices are all part of the architectural landscape that fits with the Delanys' site."

Thanks to Georgia's ability to blend various ideas and materials, the owners achieved a unique combination of mountain home, regal castle, cottage in the woods, and coastal playground. "We love the seamless merging of all these different elements," says Jim.

The cabin offers unparalleled tranquility with the constant flow of the running river.

The back-to-back-fireplaces, one in the living area and one in the screened porch, were constructed from stones found on the ruins of the old mill by the river.

In this compact cabin, the dining area is inside the screened porch, which is located just a short walk across the foyer from the kitchen.

DESIGNING WITH A PURPOSE

When designing this cabin, the Bizios architecture firm focused on keeping the structure simple so that the exterior and interior meshed seamlessly. "We wanted people to forget whether they were inside or outside," explains Georgia.

One way to do that was by giving each portion of the wraparound porch a distinct purpose. For example, the south section of the covered porch where one enters is "where they close their umbrellas, remove their muddy boots, and drop their wet coats," says Georgia. "You don't want to waste indoor space for that kind of thing. This porch area offers that 'in-between' space that is necessary and functional." It also provides a great staging area for packing and unpacking their vehicles.

On the east side, an uncovered "rocking-chair porch" offers lovely views of the pond and river. "It's a great spot to sit and listen to the river when the water is high," says Georgia. "It's also a place to plop down and read a book while catching a few rays of sunshine."

COLOR CHOICES

As for interior design, Kitty had one choice made before construction even commenced. "I'd seen a picture of a cabin in the woods with blue kitchen cabinets," says Kitty. "I knew right then I wanted blue cabinets, too!" The bold color choice works, in part because Kitty kept the room simple.

Georgia says that often people do too much in a small space, and it backfires. "You don't want to introduce too many colors, textures, and props into a room. You shouldn't paint the trim one color and the wall another," suggests Georgia. "I encourage clients to make the architecture become the background so that books, belongings, and furnishings become the focus."

UNEARTHING HISTORY

The Delanys' cabin stands on the site of an old pioneer gristmill on the Haw River. In 1887, a bridge was constructed on the property, enabling folks to come and go more easily. Pace's Mill operated until 1924, when it and the bridge were destroyed by a tornado. The old piers still stand in the river.

The passing of years, as well as the elements, have buried a number of artifacts. Since purchasing the property, however, the Delanys have uncovered a good bit of history. They have used some of the millstones to restore walls along the river, and repurposed others as tables and decorative pieces.

In addition to millstones, Jim and Kitty have unearthed 40–50 iron and metal machinery objects, such as pins, spikes, gears, and gate mechanisms—all part of the 1,500-pound turbines that implemented the mill's hydropower.

"Currently, we have the nicer pieces displayed on our mantel," says Jim.

BOTH ISOLATION AND CONVENIENCE

The cabin offers unparalleled tranquility with the constant flow of the running river. There is also the early-morning sound of geese and ducks; at night, there's the crazy-loud frog chorus. The Delanys regularly spot bald eagles, herons, wild turkeys, and ospreys. (A friend brings night-vision goggles when he visits so they can glimpse nocturnal minks.)

Aside from the water and the wildlife, the owners don't have to contend with many noises. Their closest neighbors are a third of a mile away. "The property is very private with no development on the river to speak of, and parcels on the river are in the hundreds of acres," says Kitty.

Perched 130 feet above the 500-foot-wide riverbank, the owners reap the benefit of the land's unique topography: their very own "microclimate" created by cool, moist air rising off the water and the angle of the sun on the hillside. Such conditions encourage an atypical growth of mountain laurel. (According to Jim, another patch can't be found for another 50–100 miles.)

Despite being tucked away, the owners are actually close to civilization. "It feels like we're in the middle of the mountains," says Jim. "And yet, just fifteen minutes away we have five-star restaurants."

Not that the family dines out much. They prefer to gather in the screened porch for meals at their dining room table, which seats up to twelve. "If it's chilly, we move the table in front of the outdoor fireplace," says Kitty. "We even hosted Thanksgiving at the cabin one year."

FAMILY TIME

The Delanys' sons, Newman and Chance, both attended UNC–Chapel Hill, enabling them to enjoy the family cabin—not to mention the laundering facilities.

"It's been nice to have the boys drop by for breakfast or dinner," says Kitty. "Chance sometimes brings buddies, and they go fly-fishing. He also uses the cabin for a quiet place to study."

The family has had pig roasts, marshmallow roasts, and countless fireside chats with friends. They even built a bocce court by the river to have a fun game for people to enjoy at the mill site. Kitty's favorite cabin pastime is curling up with a good book. "I love to read, but at home I feel like I should be doing something constructive," says Kitty. "I never feel guilty reading at the cabin." She and Jim also take walks, play golf, and just unwind on the river's edge.

"Honestly, I'm not sure we'll ever build the main house," notes Kitty. "This cabin suits our needs perfectly!" ■

With this cabin, the square footage of the outdoor living spaces exceeds that of the indoor spaces.

A funky old summer camp makes way for a family retreat that fits beautifully into its surroundings and captures lake views from every room.

"I WANTED THE WHOLE LAKE SIDE OF OUR HOME OPEN TO THE WATER."

A CABIN DESIGNED FOR PRIME VIEWS

Suzy Kerr describes her spot on Vermont's Lake Fairlee in terms we can all understand. "Lake Fairlee looks like a kidney bean, and we're at the part of the bean that dents in," she explains. "Our property is pie shaped with the crust facing the shoreline."

Suzy and her husband, Gordon, purchased a rustic 800-square-foot cabin right at the water's edge on Passumpsic Point. The property was a former summer camp for boys. And while these primitive quarters had been passable for the two of them, augmented with a guest cabin, the Kerrs wanted a vacation place suitable to host their children and grandchildren.

"It really was a funky old camp with no foundation and not intended for year-round use," recalls the couple's architect, Pi Smith. "It just wasn't worth it." So with the renovation dreams dashed, the team at Smith & Vansant Architects in Norwich, Vermont, went to work designing the Kerrs' new getaway.

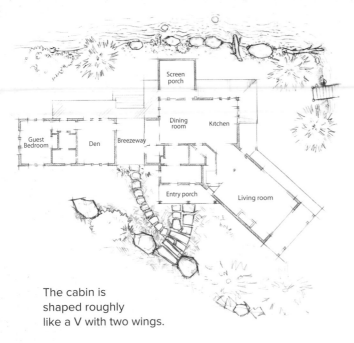

The cabin is shaped roughly like a V with two wings.

The stairway has paddle-themed balusters.

And then came the phone call. "They'd decided to take this from a weekend cabin to a permanent residence for retirement," says Smith. This changed everything.

A CABIN SHAPED LIKE A V

The firm now had to design on a bigger scale, while still respecting the constants driving the project. While the lake home needed to be large enough for year-round living, the Kerrs didn't want a McMansion that would dominate the landscape.

"The old camp went right up on the shoreline, and for many reasons, I personally don't think you should encroach the water," says Suzy. That being said, Smith was challenged to maximize water views on a uniquely shaped property, while shielding views of neighboring cabins.

To satisfy these concerns, the retreat is roughly shaped like a V; its two wings have decks and porches on each side to capture the sunrise and sunset. At the center of the V is a two-story, New England–style gable house with a first-floor kitchen and dining room, and a master suite above. A single-story living room makes up one wing of the V, capturing a stunning angled view of the water.

Back at the center of the V are a laundry room and a vestibule that flows into a fifteen-foot breezeway, open to the elements. This is a pause before the other wing—a smaller guest area known as "the bunkhouse" with a bedroom, den, and bath.

The breezeway also provides a buffer from noise and a side entrance into the home, while making this wing truly a separate location that can be closed off when not in use. Another benefit is enhanced curb appeal. "When you drive up to the building, you see the water through the breezeway, so the building is a little bit porous feeling, not like a dam blocking off the lake," says Smith.

Every room in the house
has a water view.

The built-ins include kitchen-island bookshelves (above) and a master bathroom window seat (below).

Because really, no matter how lovely the cabin is, it's all about the lake, right?

EVERY ROOM HAS A VIEW

When designing, every effort was made to capitalize on views while making it easy to step out into them. Keeping the living spaces as low to the lake as possible, while strategically orienting the main rooms to block views of neighboring homes, Smith's design makes the retreat seem like it's entirely surrounded by water.

She explains that by setting the whole structure at an angle to the water, it took on unobstructed diagonal sightlines. "Every room in the house has a water view," says Smith. Best of all, the new place allows the family to enjoy the sunrise on the east patio. "We didn't even know we could see the sunrise on our property," says Suzy. For views like these, the couple was willing to make some concessions. "I gave up a lot of cabinets for that view; I wanted the whole lake side of our home open to the water," says Suzy.

Lastly, Smith designed so many windows that the rooms feel bigger and convey the sense that one is outside in the trees.

STEPPING OUT

Getting out to all this tempting scenery is easy in a home surrounded with a wraparound deck, a covered porch that cascades onto the stone terrace, and a sensational summer dining room. "All of these outdoor elements connect to each other with steps to everything," says Smith, who used these open-air rooms to lure guests outdoors. This easy transition from indoor to out has really enhanced the way the Kerrs use their lake place.

"People peel out all the doors—there are so many entrances, all drawing you to the water," says Suzy. And by pulling the cabin back from the shoreline, the Kerrs acquired more yard on the lake side of their cabin—space for a lakefront patio, comfy chairs, and lawn games. "We really live out there."

THE SWEET SPOT

Perhaps the sweetest spot in the house for family gatherings is the screened-in porch, positioned with water on three sides to capture views and sun to the west, south, and east. And with doors leading to it from inside the house and from decks on two sides, one could say it's the heart of the cabin.

Now that two of the Kerrs' grandchildren are old enough to attend summer camp on the lake, this porch is the perfect spot to watch for them. "There's nothing like sitting out there and watching the grandkids canoe by our home and wave," says Suzy.

The patio is off of the living room.

BLENDING IN

Much thought went into making the home visually friendly to those out on Lake Fairlee, as well. The center gable's style echoes the region's century-old architecture, with its classic dark-brown shingle exterior and green trim blending into the property's tall pines. Also, to minimize the impression of size, rooflines were kept intentionally low. And, Suzy says, "From the water, one can never see both wings at the same time." These extra efforts have been worth it. "We get so many nice comments from paddlers," she says.

I JUST MIGHT KNOW A GUY

When it came to making the inside special, the Kerrs got some help from their builder, Chip Odell ("a man who knows a guy," says Suzy). Through a series of special connections with hunters, woodsmen, and collectors, Chip got hold of some hemlock flooring from a classic New England inn's casino game room. This reclaimed wood is now laid throughout the Kerr's home, making it feel like the place has always been there.

Because the family was nearing the top of their budget, Chip had a great idea for the bathroom vanity. By distressing pieces of pine board, the inexpensive wood fit right in with the rustic hemlock flooring.

"A story I love telling is about a bet placed by Chip on exactly when we'd notice the stonework," says Suzy. Chip had convinced a skilled mason to build the Kerr's fireplace. "It took us two months to notice the shapes of Vermont and New Hampshire laid in the fireplace," Suzy admits, "even after we spent so much time in the room painting all the walls ourselves!" And though the mason denies it, the Kerrs say they can clearly see his initials in the stonework, too. "It was his last fireplace ever. Who can blame him?" Not the Kerrs. ■

THE COZY CABIN

One of *Cabin Living* magazine's most popular issues is the annual "Small Cabin Issue." The genesis of modern America's enduring fondness for small home living is often linked to Sarah Susanka's book *The Not So Big House: A Blueprint for the Way We Really Live*, which first published in 1998. Just as in Susanka's books, a common theme of the cozy cabin stories that follow is making the most of small spaces.

The cabin's exterior includes siding elements that are nicely suited to a smaller scale.

"IT OOZED VINTAGE CHARM BUT WAS OUTLIVING ITS TIME."

FROM SOMETHING OLD TO SOMETHING NEW

Originally from the Northeast, Lynn Wachter grew up vacationing at her great-grandfather's cottage on Fire Island, a barrier island in the Atlantic off the coast of New York. She hoped that one day she, too, would own a tranquil getaway.

In 2002, her dream was realized when she and her husband, Steve, bought a 750-square-foot cabin on Goodrich Lake in Crosslake, Minnesota. Although Lynn immediately fell in love with the Northwoods atmosphere, she wanted to pull more light into the dark-green interior to recreate the airy ambiance of her grandfather's beach cottage.

But ambiance would have to wait, since at the time the family didn't have the resources to renovate. They did, however, snatch up the adjacent hundred-foot lot with a 450-square-foot mini-cottage. With bunk beds, bathroom, small kitchen, and screened porch, it was well suited for guests.

The owners used the footprint of the old deck to create the master bedroom and front entry.

Bedroom furniture (the nightstands, bed, and dresser) came from IKEA.

PASSING THE TIME

Since Crosslake is only 150 miles from the Wachters' main residence in Edina, Minnesota, the family uses their retreat in all four seasons. It sees the most action, though, in summer, when the gang takes to the water. Of course, swimming, kayaking, and canoeing work up an appetite.

"I'd say that 50 percent of what we do there is grilling," says Steve. "The other 50 percent is probably spent floating—either on our pontoon or on our inflatable party island." With built-in seats and cupholders, the giant raft is the ideal spot for rest and relaxation. "We'll float all day long with friends and a well-stocked cooler," says Steve, noting that invariably somebody has to retrieve the island with the pontoon once it has drifted too far out.

A FORMER FISHING CAMP

In addition to boating and floating, the lake offers great bass fishing. In fact, the original cabin was part of a seasonal fishing camp. Erected in 1946, it was modified through the years with several clunky additions and questionable installations. Over time, sections of the structure had deteriorated beyond repair. "It oozed vintage charm but was outliving its time," explains Steve.

After debating whether they should sell the property or renovate the existing structure, the family decided to take the cabin down to the studs and use the footprint of the deck to create a master bedroom and front entry.

To make it a year-round getaway, the Wachters rebuilt with full insulation, new roof, walls, siding and windows, along with a full HVAC system with air exchanger. A new partial basement, accessed by a floor hatch in the entryway, serves as a mechanical room and storage.

The back
of the cabin
features a deck
for outdoor
entertaining.

The couple also added a second bathroom, and created a more spacious kitchen by removing the woodstove in the living room and eliminating a small bedroom. Ultimately, they added 150 square feet, bringing the total living space to 900 square feet.

ARCHITECTURAL DESIGN CHALLENGES

In retrospect, the owners admit that they probably should have completely rebuilt the cabin.

"Remodels are always challenging because you're taking the original bones of a cabin that was built fifty or sixty years ago and merging it with a new structure," says Matt Balmer, co-owner of Lands End Development in nearby Crosslake. The company designed the new floor plan and executed the remodel. "Marrying up an old

The bathroom mirror in closed position.

The mirror opens to let air into the bathroom.

The washer and dryer fit neatly in a closet.

foundation with a new foundation is hard enough as you ensure the framing is straight, but then you don't want to lose the charm of the original cabin. It's a tricky process."

But the Wachters were afraid if they tore it down, they wouldn't be allowed to build on the same footprint due to zoning issues. "On this project, one of the parameters of the small lot and the local zoning was that the footprint could only be expanded minimally," explains Jeff Balmer, Lands End co-owner and lead designer. "So we had to get creative with the space we had."

When faced with this constraint, Jeff decided that the best location for the master bath was on the road side of the cabin. Although this choice worked fine with the interior layout, it posed a dilemma. Without windows to balance the ones by the entry, a blank wall could detract from the appeal of the facade. And while Lynn welcomed the prospect of natural light, she wasn't thrilled about the accompanying lack of privacy. Jeff's solution was ingenious. First, he built a bump-out

"NOW I LOVE EVERY NOOK AND CRANNY OF THIS PLACE."

with a twin-unit window for the vanity area, then fashioned a pair of interior mirrored shutters. Closing the shutters provides a mirror above the vanity; from the outside, only a reflection of the property's pine trees is visible.

AN AIRY, COLORFUL RETREAT

Eager to replicate her great-grandpa's coastal cottage, Lynn stained the cedar shakes gray and painted the front door turquoise blue. For the interior, Lynn chose colors to suit the beach style she craved, including more turquoise, white, orange, and terra-cotta.

"I wanted the interior to be light and bright since Minnesota has a long, dark winter season," says Lynn. "Now I love every nook and cranny of this place."

"And I love having central air-conditioning!" pipes in Steve, quick to point out that despite rumors to the contrary, Minnesota summers can be warm and humid.

The owners' Australian shepherd loves riding in the pontoon.

The Wachters completely redid the kitchen. "The peninsula is always the congregation point for company!" says Steve.

A HAVEN FOR EVERY SEASON

Both love relaxing on the new wraparound deck with their dog, an Australian shepherd named Allie. They're often joined by friends and family, including grown sons Trevor and Bryan, and Bryan's wife, Shannon. The clan enjoys playing a host of yard games like disc golf, cornhole (aka beanbag toss), and "the crazy homemade ones that only college kids know," says Lynn. When in a mood to venture out, they bike the back roads or head to the quaint resort town of Crosslake, five miles away. Brimming with souvenir shops, miniature golf courses, tasty ice cream parlors, and a general store that sells the essentials, it's the "just big enough yet not too big" kind of town, says Lynn.

While the Wachters don't spend as much time at the lake during the bitter cold months, they relish winter getaways for the snowshoeing, ice-skating, and cross-country skiing opportunities on the cabin doorstep.

"When the lake freezes over, it's like we own an extra 400 acres," says Steve, who crafts his own winter wonderland by stringing white twinkle lights along the property.

THE BEAUTY OF SIMPLICITY

After years of cottage ownership, the Wachters have made an observation about cottage/cabin living: Even the bad memories are good. For instance, there's the time when they had a houseful of guests and lost power during a brutal heat wave. "It was too hot to sleep inside, so everyone spread out on the grass with the chiggers and mosquitoes and kept the good times rolling," recalls Lynn. Despite sweaty bodies and itchy skin, the humid air was filled with campfire smoke, bug repellent, and hearty laughter.

Steve says that it's obvious why everyone was in such good spirits. "People are just thrilled to be at the cabin." ■

The owners achieved their cabin dream over time as they could afford to do so. They built this tiny 196-square-foot cabin before erecting their main cabin.

THE AFFORDABLE LOG CABIN

Instant gratification seems to be an obsession for many people these days. But then there are cabin owners like Kristi and Mike Portugue, who took fifteen years to fully achieve their dream.

CATCHING THE CABIN BUG

For both these native Minnesotans, cabin living was a big part of growing up in the Land of 10,000 Lakes.

Kristi's parents rented a cabin every summer at The Nifty Nook Resort on Otter Tail Lake in west-central Minnesota. Mike's folks owned a cabin on Side Lake in the northern part of the state.

After meeting in college in St. Paul, the couple visited The Nifty Nook once a year and the Portugue family cabin throughout the summer. The tradition continued into their married life.

CABIN LIVING CROSSROADS

But Kristi's parents stopped renting at Nifty Nook in the early- to mid-1990s, and Mike's parents sold their cabin in the late '90s. By that time,

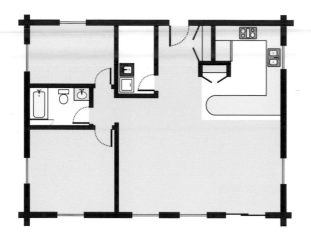

The shell of the 1,760-square-foot main cabin has a simple floor plan, with a kitchen, great room/dining area, two bedrooms, bathroom, and utility room. (A spacious loft area is not shown on the plan.)

The cabin has a eagle's-nest-like view of the lake below.

Kristi and Mike were proud owners of two active Portuguese water dogs who loved the lake country.

The couple was at a crossroads. "We had the dogs and wanted somewhere to go with them, not just go on trips and leave them behind while we traveled," Kristi says.

PURCHASING THE LAND

The solution? They would build their own cabin on a lake. After an extensive search, the Portugues bought a three-acre parcel in Minnesota's northeastern Arrowhead region in December 2001. The land is near Ely, a short distance from the Boundary Waters Canoe Area Wilderness. "It was quiet and peaceful," Kristi reflects. On the lake side, the property is shielded by an island. There is also privacy on the road side. "You can't see the neighbors," notes Mike.

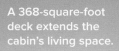

A 368-square-foot deck extends the cabin's living space.

Mike and Kristi frequently host family and friends at their getaway.

"The atmosphere is just so . . . simple, quiet, slower," says Mike.

There's a Zodiac inflatable for fishing and puttering on the lake—the dogs love it!

FIRST THINGS FIRST

From the outset, the couple decided to build in stages as funds allowed.

Part of the property is a rocky peninsula with a 180-degree view of the lake. The shoreline falls away to deep water, perfect for docking boats, swimming, and fishing. A septic system wasn't allowed on the peninsula, and the Portugues decided to forgo the luxuries of power and running water as well. But a tiny log cabin in this ideal location was the perfect starting point for this budget-conscious couple.

There was just one major hurdle: access. The rocky point is separated from the rest of the property by a wetland. So in 2002, the couple built a boardwalk over a base of railroad ties. "It was a challenging project!" Mike recalls. "We built it with the help of my dad, Jerry, who was 65 years old at the time, Kristi's father, Ordean, 77, and her mother, Dorothy, 75."

DECIDING ON LOG CONSTRUCTION

When weighing cabin construction options, Mike and Kristi agreed on log. "The terrain is so wild and natural that it seemed that log would fit well there," says Kristi.

"I just wanted the total cabin feel," Mike notes, "not just a second home on a lake."

First, they looked at a local provider of manufactured logs. "But they were expensive, and the logs were smaller than we wanted, even for the little cabin," he recalls. "And then we found Brian Kainz." The craftsman's log yard was just down the road from the property. And as luck would have it, Kainz had enough logs left over from another project for a tiny getaway.

"We liked the idea of building with handcrafted logs because they'd look more rustic and natural," Kristi says.

The great room/dining area looks out to the deck and the lake.

"The craftsmanship of hand-scribing logs with no gaps and no chinking is incredible," adds Mike.

BUILDING AND LIVING IN A LIL' CABIN

The design was "based on plans we had seen over time in magazines," Kristi explains. "We sited it for views of the lake."

The shell of the 14 x 14-foot structure was erected in May; by September, it was mostly finished. The one-room retreat held a futon, dresser, table and chairs, plus a loft that could be used for either sleeping or storage. Mike built a 256-square-foot deck the following May.

The Portugues enjoyed their off-grid getaway, hauling water from home in five-gallon jugs and cooking on a propane camp stove on the deck. Upon arrival, they'd cart luggage and water jugs down the boardwalk in a wheelbarrow. With an outdoor living space larger than indoor, meal prep, cooking, and dishes were typically handled on the deck. A propane camp stove and grill supplied the cooking space, while a Coleman Hot Water On Demand H2Oasis Portable Water heater supplied hot water for dishwashing. Mike also built an outdoor sun shower for al fresco bathing.

MOVING ON UP

Eventually, the time was right to start building the main cabin on the highest portion of their property. "Kainz told us he knew of a stand of forty- to fifty-foot-tall red pine in Isabella [Minnesota.]. He said it was a close-growing stand, so the logs would be great for a cabin," Mike recalls.

An open-plan design was drawn up by brother-in-law Mike Wilkus of Wilkus Architecture in the Twin Cities. (Mike is married to Kristi's older sister, Barb.) Mat Roderick of Evergreen Construction in Ely signed on as contractor.

In the kitchen, the cabinets and beadboard are painted red with a black glaze. Barn lights illuminate the countertop.

In October, the building site was excavated and a slab poured, complete with provisions for future hookups for plumbing and a radiant-floor heating system.

A flatbed semi-trailer truck delivered the logs the following June, and the shell was erected.

THE MAIN CABIN SLOWLY COMES TOGETHER

The design called for 1,200 square feet on the main floor plus a 560-square-foot loft. The cabin came together slowly over the next year or so, becoming more and more livable along the way.

Meanwhile, the Portugues focused on saving funds for the finishing touches.

Next, Roderick's crew built a 368-square-foot deck overlooking the lake; two years later, they added a deck/walkway to the main entry on the opposite side of the cabin. All Day Builders based in Ely installed a large flagstone patio with a grill area, fire pit, and outdoor shower between the decks. The lakeside deck has a hefty high-top outdoor dining table with great sightlines to the lake plus a cozy outdoor seating area for dining, reading a magazine, or enjoying a chat.

A REAL KITCHEN AND BATHROOM—AT LAST!

The span of two years brought the final comforts of home to the main cabin: a real kitchen to replace the temporary one, a septic system and a bathroom, along with a well, washer/dryer, and dishwasher.

For the kitchen and bath, Kristi called on her sister Carol Johnson, a designer for AB&K Remodeling in Milwaukee. The result was the culmination of years of planning that had started in 2006. "We worked slowly on the plan, meeting over a few summers with sample options and potential cabinet layouts. Then we utilized technology to send ideas and plans back and forth since we live about 400 miles from each other," says Johnson.

The kitchen features sleek red cabinets with a black glaze. "This choice contrasts nicely with the warm log walls and ceiling," explains Johnson. The couple opted for maintenance-free high-definition laminate countertops. A glass-and-stone mosaic tiled wall lends sparkle.

Instead of a tub in the small bathroom, the Portugues decided on a large tiled shower. The slate-look tile floor and shower surround offset warm cherry cabinetry, designed to maximize storage.

ON THE EDGE OF THE WILDERNESS

The Portugues' playground begins on the 465-acre lake but extends to the surrounding wilderness area and the outdoorsy town of Ely.

"The change between our life in the Twin Cities and here is 180 degrees different," says Mike. The atmosphere is just so . . . simple, quiet, slower. You just appreciate things more, like at night how dark dark can really be, especially down at the little cabin."

"Every day is kind of like an adventure every time we get to the cabin," says Kristi. The Portugues' "fleet" attests to the fact that this family enjoys a variety of water sports: barefooting, waterskiing, wakeboarding, and more. Besides the Sanger barefoot ski boat, there's a Zodiac inflatable for fishing and puttering on the lake; rowboats for training the dogs in their water-trial work; standup paddleboards, kayaks, and a canoe.

When not on the water, the Portugues might be found on the long access road riding bikes or walking the dogs (The tribe of Portuguese water dogs has expanded to three: Moby, Hydro, and Sprite). They also venture into the surrounding wilderness area, hiking beside pristine lakes or magnificent waterfalls.

Mike and Kristi frequently host family and friends at their getaway, in groups small and large.

With a guest bedroom and an expansive loft, the main cabin can easily sleep six to eight. The tiny cabin can sleep an additional four, and there's space for pitching a tent.

When all Mike and Kristi had was the little cabin on the peninsula, Mike called it "The Shack." Now that the couple has finished the main cabin, Mike refers to their entire property as "The Shack."

Kristi laughs, but disagrees: "It's 'The *Cabin*.'"

Whatever you call the Portugues' little slice of paradise on the edge of the wilderness, it was well worth the wait. ■

This outdoorsy Tennessee cabin—
designed to look like it was built in
the 1850s—might be small,
but it lives large.

"A SMALL HOUSE IS MORE LIVABLE THAN YOU MIGHT THINK."

COZY MEETS RUSTIC

Why would someone who builds cabins for a living want to shoehorn his own large family into a log cabin with only an 18 x 24 footprint?

In Randy Giles's case, chalk it up to stubbornness. "It was an exercise in trying to build small and live small," says Giles, owner of Hearthstone Homes, a timber frame and log homebuilder in Newport, Tennessee. "That was important to me. I wanted to say, 'Yes, I can build a livable cabin that is this small.'"

RAISING A FAMILY, CREATING MEMORIES

And for fifteen years, Randy and his wife, Toni, made it work—even as the family grew to include the first four of their five children.

Of course, it didn't hurt that the cabin sits on eighty acres beside Douglas Lake in Tennessee. The children grew up on the water and learned to boat at an early age. Sometimes they spent the night on the lake in the boat. They camped out in three seasons. A small house creates more motivation for everyone in the family to pursue outdoor activities, Giles found.

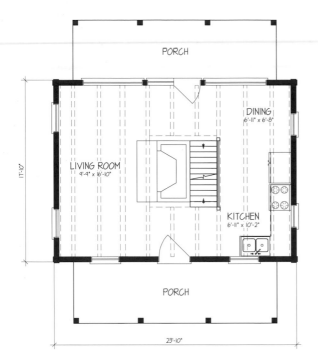

The floor plan included porches on both sides of the cabin.

One departure from 1800s' style is the large picture window to bring in the light and outdoor vistas.

"I don't know whether living in a log house makes you feel outdoorsy or whether people who enjoy the outdoors are drawn to cabin living," he says. "The kids weren't intent on sleeping in a bed every night."

Because of the small kitchen, the family ate many meals out on the porch—something they relished but might not have done if they'd lived in a larger house.

GENESIS OF THE DREAM

Let's start at the beginning: Giles grew up in Pennsylvania, and after four years at Purdue University on the plains of Indiana, he hankered to return to gentle, tree-covered mountains. In the early 1980s, he came across a forested property in the Smoky Mountain foothills near Dandridge. The panorama overlooking Douglas Lake was priceless. "Access to the lake and the view were compensating factors," Giles says. "If you want to live on a spectacular ridge or beside a mountain lake, building on a steep lot may be the only way to do it."

Giles used antique heart pine, recycled from homes built generations ago.

The modular fireplace has an indoor chimney that serves as a masonry radiator, capturing heat as the smoke wends its way out the roof.

The cabin's décor is simple and uncluttered.

He saved the prime building spot for the dream house he wanted to build someday.

For the starter home that he would build immediately, he scouted out a site on the cusp of where the land dropped precipitously to the lake. There, in 1985, he constructed his three-story, 1,200-square-foot log cabin. The main level encompassed the family's living space, with a small kitchen and dining area. Giles added a master bedroom-and-bath suite in an enclosed loft above the main living area.

And because the cabin is built on a slope, the topography allowed for a walkout basement with windows on three sides. Giles built another bedroom-and-bath suite there for the children.

Historical connections matter to Giles. He wanted the cabin to look as if it had been on the site for 150 years, though it could not be an exact replica. People were smaller generations ago, so a cabin from that period would have smaller doors; heating was primitive, resulting in the need for smaller windows. But Giles paid attention to the height of the cabin, the pitch of the roof, the construction materials, and, of course, the porches.

RETHINK COSTS

A small retreat has all of the expensive, fixed-cost spaces—a kitchen and baths—and fewer inexpensive discretionary spaces such as hallways and large rooms to offset the cost-per-square-foot price. A $20,000 fireplace will have a greater impact on the cost-per-square-foot of an 800-square-foot house than on a 3,000-square-foot house. But, the total cost of a small house may be less.

IMPORTANCE OF THE PORCH

"The smaller the house, the more important the porches are," Giles says. "Porches create extra living space."

The front porch in Giles's cabin is only six feet wide, authentic to cabins at the time when pioneers were frugal with space and timber.

Giles added a back porch to take advantage of the lake view and the spectacular sunsets. The back porch accommodates a generous dining table, and the family often ate outdoors or used the space for entertaining.

About eight years ago, Giles strayed slightly from strict adherence to reproduction by replacing two small windows that opened onto the back porch with a large section of fixed glass. He cut out some of the logs and reframed the section in timber. Now, the view across the lake welcomes people as soon as they walk through the front door. The retrofit makes the house feel so much bigger, he adds.

The Giles children grew up on the water. Built on an eighty-acre site overlooking Douglas Lake, the cabin lived large in part due to its expansive surroundings.

"PORCHES CREATE EXTRA LIVING SPACE."

What better way to catch the cooling breezes in summer and expand the living space than a porch?

LEANING TOWARD ECLECTIC

Having built many cabins for customers over the years, Giles has observed a trend toward the eclectic. When he started out in the 1970s, customers valued authenticity more than anything. But today's cabin owner isn't afraid to take design liberties. People may want the front of the cabin to look like a traditional old log home, but the interior will often feature an open floor plan with lots of glass to maximize outdoor vistas and brighten the cabin.

Giles experimented with placing the fireplace in the middle of the room rather than on an outside wall. An exterior chimney would have allowed more living space but would also lose heat to the outdoors. He challenged himself by installing a modular fireplace. (Usually sold in kits, modular, pre-built masonry fireplaces are lighter and less costly than site-built fireplaces.) An indoor chimney served as a masonry radiator, capturing heat as the smoke wended its way out the roof.

"The technology reflected a centuries-old technique used in northern Europe and northern Asia of sending the smoke out on a circuitous route to extract heat before it left the house," Giles explains.

QUALITY MATERIALS IN A SMALL CABIN

What Giles sacrificed in space, he made up for in quality. With less square footage, he could spend more on antique heart pine, used liberally throughout the cabin. The floors, stairs, cabinetry, and door were made from the reclaimed wood.

UNEXPECTED BENEFITS

Living as a family in a compact space yielded some unexpected benefits for the Giles crew: Everyone felt less inclined to accumulate things and more motivated to keep the place tidy.

"A small house has built-in brakes on clutter," Giles says. "Where are you going to walk if you have stuff everywhere?"

The Giles family lived in the compact cabin for fifteen years before Giles built a larger home on the land's premier site. (In case you're wondering, the original cabin is very much in demand by visiting friends and family.)

Giles looks back fondly at the good times the family shared in the cabin. In fact, he and his oldest son both write songs, and many originate from memories they have of cabin life on the lake.

Looking back, Giles is satisfied that his exercise in living small succeeded. "The small cabin worked amazingly well for an amazingly long time," he says. "A small house is more livable than you might think." ■

Nestled into a mature forest and overlooking a lake, this petite home is a classic portrait of the ideal Montana cabin.

WHAT MORE DO YOU NEED?

Some celebrities are notorious for building cabins with scant consideration for the landscape or the local traditions. This is especially true in Montana, where Hollywood heroes are known to buy up ranches and build multimillion-dollar vacation homes.

Not so in the case of Jack Hanna and his wife, Suzi. The world-renowned wildlife expert and television personality is best known as host of the show *Jack Hanna's into the Wild*, as well as for many guest spots on *Good Morning America* and other talk shows. But Hanna doesn't consider himself a celebrity, despite what others might say. "I don't like the word," he says. "I don't like the word 'star,' either. I don't like any of those words. That's not me." (If you must call him something, he prefers "Animal Ambassador"; Jack and Suzi devote much of the year to traveling the globe on behalf of wildlife conservation.)

Hanna could easily have gone the same mega-lodge route as others when he decided to buy property outside Big Fork, Montana. But that just wouldn't be his style.

"A lot of times, people in these small communities see people like me moving in and think,

The owners have seen elk, moose, wolf, black bear, and mountain lions from their porch.

Part of the appeal of a true log cabin is the timelessness of the design.

'Oh gosh, what's he going to do?'" he says. "Well, I tell you what. I have a little farm up there—it's a farm, not a ranch—on forty acres." Born and raised on a farm in Tennessee, Hanna tends chickens, cows, and goats on his Montana spread. But only in the summer. "Because we're not there year-round, we rent the animals," he says. "The grandkids love it. They pet the cows and play with the goats. Did you know you can rent eight chickens for fifty dollars for the summer?"

The property also has, Hanna continues, "some trails and a few small cabins for my family." Jack and Suzi have three children and several grandchildren, all of whom enjoy gathering here whenever possible. And when he says small, he's not kidding. Coming in at just 700 square feet, the Elk Cabin is truly petite. But really, argues Hanna, what more do you need? "When we were building it, we really didn't know what we were doing. But I figured, hey, it's a cabin—four walls, one room downstairs, a loft upstairs, put a kitchen in, and that's it."

"THERE'S NO BETTER PLACE IN THE WORLD TO GO HIKING THAN GLACIER NATIONAL PARK."

Designed and built by a stonemason using traditional techniques, the fireplace provides a striking focal point for the interior.

A claw-foot bathtub highlights the historic feel of the cabin.

With an efficient kitchen, utilitarian furnishings, and a tiny footprint, simplicity rules the day at this cabin.

RENT-A-CHICKEN

You don't need to be a professional zookeeper like Jack Hanna to keep a petting zoo at your retreat. From coast to coast, barnyard animals are available to rent in most parts of Cabin Country. Just think: fresh eggs for breakfast, a goat to mow the lawn while you go fishing. And the best part is, like the grandkids, you can hold 'em and then give them back!

AN ADVENTURE IN BUILDING

Builder Randy Baker concurs with the apparent simplicity and humility of the Hannas' aesthetic. He can also relate to the somewhat haphazard approach they took when building this, the second cabin on the property. It must be noted that Baker, like Hanna, also prefers a different kind of title. "I always tell Jack, 'I'm not a carpenter.' And he says, 'Yeah, okay, right, you're not a carpenter.' And I say, 'No, I'm a handyman. But I think we can figure this carpentry thing out.' "

Over the course of a twenty-year relationship with Hanna (and several cabins later), Baker admits that maybe he's figured a few things out. He enjoys recounting the process of building the Elk Cabin in 1996: "Jack called me up and said, 'The guys from Logcrafters are on their way up, and they're bringing logs.' So they brought a crane up to stack them, and then we're building this thing, and we'd actually gotten most of it done. I'm sitting up there on the roof one day, and Jack shows up. He pulls this tube out of the truck and says, 'Well, obviously you don't need these.' And I say, 'What's that, Jack?' And he says, 'Well, they're the plans!' See, they didn't leave me any plans. We were just winging it the whole project. So he put them back in the truck and that was the end of the plans. We never did see them."

Luckily, Baker's handyman skills and common sense proved up to the task. Two decades later, the Elk Cabin is as sturdy and charming as ever. Made of locally harvested and hewn timbers, it is truly the quintessential log cabin. Simply outfitted, the rustic furnishings and sparse decorations let the warm wood interior speak for itself. Quilts and blankets invite cozy relaxation. Tucked among the trees, the secluded hideaway boasts a beautiful, meticulously built fireplace, an old-fashioned claw-foot tub, and a comfy porch overlooking cherry orchards.

While some people prefer fancy accommodations, the owners are content with a loft bedroom, a log bed frame, and a forest view.

WHY MONTANA?

So why would a globetrotter like Jack Hanna build his retirement home way up in the corner of Montana? "I've traveled the world—South America, Africa, Australia," says Hanna. "But the reason we chose Montana is very simple: I love the people, I love the climate all four seasons of the year—and more than anything, my wife and I love hiking. There's no better place in the world to go hiking than Glacier National Park."

Then there's the proximity to Flathead Lake. And for Hanna, what could be better than the local version of *Into the Wild*, up close and personal? "We've had elk, moose, wolf, black bears, mountain lions, and there's been a bald eagle nest there for the past three years," he says.

Hanna admits that some of his friends are a little baffled by his penchant for the place, especially since he's been returning year after year for decades. "They ask me, 'Gosh, what do you do out there? It's the middle of nowhere!'" he says. "But you know, I've been going out there since 1984. That's thirty years, and I've still only done 10 percent of the things I want to do. There's so much more. Montana takes a lifetime to discover, and that's what I intend to do." ■

Locally harvested timbers make up the majority of the cabin. No wonder it blends so nicely with its surroundings.

This little Big Sky cabin was built to fit its owner just right.

"I DIDN'T WANT THE
CLICHÉ RUSTIC."

COZY
MOUNTAIN
CABIN

If you ask Paul Larson whether he has a favorite
room or feature in his Kalispell, Montana, cabin,
he'll tell you, "Yes, definitely. I love the big patio
door in the living room," he says, referencing
the three-panel glass door that opens onto the
wraparound porch. "And the loft bedroom," he
continues. "And the porch too, of course. And the
kitchen. Oh, and the radiant-floor heat!"

CABIN-BUILDING SUCCESS

When a homeowner counts nearly every facet of
his cabin among his favorite features, it's a good
indication that the building process was a success
from conception to execution. But Paul is quick
to point out that the success wasn't the result of
happenstance or luck. Rather, it was the product of a clear vision and good communication
from the outset. "Paul is specific and helpful,"
notes designer/builder Jason Gerbozy of J Martin
Builders in Kalispell. "It's fun to work with someone who knows exactly what they want."

Larson designed his home around the basics, which enabled him to keep it small.

Yet, he didn't skimp either. A fully appointed kitchen is plenty big for two to work comfortably.

SMALL CABIN DESIGN

"It sounds silly," Paul admits, "but I actually designed this house around specific furniture." Although enamored of the tiny-house movement, Paul knew that a true tiny house wasn't for him. Still, the basic tenets of the movement—simplicity, deliberateness of design, economy of space—informed the cabin's roughly 1,000-square-foot design.

The decision-making process was all about tough, thoughtful choices. "I had the stuff that I knew I needed and wanted to be in the cabin," he explains. "And I didn't want any more space than was needed to fit those pieces. It was all very practical." As a result, each room feels perfectly furnished. The sofa is just the right size to demarcate living room from kitchen. The dining table nestles comfortably into the dining nook. An upstairs workstation hosts a desk, chair, and bookshelf—no more, no less.

ROOM TO BREATHE

And while small cabins can often feel cramped, such is not the case here. Although the design is space-conscious, nothing has been compromised. Everything is full-feature, with full-size appliances and fixtures. Banks of windows; high, pine-paneled ceilings; and neutral colors contribute to the spacious feel, as do streamlined modern features

The stacked-wood staircase
is the perfect blend of rustic
materials in a modern context.

A clever built-in doghouse under the stairs provides the perfect canine hideout.

Larson's dog, Ivan, emerges from his nap.

LIVING LARGE IN A SMALL CABIN

Houses with a small footprint can often feel even smaller than they are, based on the choices the homeowner or designer makes. Undersizing features like doors and fixtures can sometimes highlight the cramped nature of the space, rather than mask it. So how to overcome this problem? It's all a matter of camouflage, according to builder Jason Gerbozy of J Martin Builders, Kalispell, Montana.

For instance, a storage space in the second-floor loft required a door—but the space couldn't accommodate a full-size door, and a truncated one would have looked awkward. Instead, Jason's builders devised a bookcase door instead, which appears to be a normal shelf but also provides access to the storage space behind.

like metal railings and simple cabinetry. "A lot of my preferences were things that I had seen elsewhere," says Paul, stressing the importance of extensive brainstorming and research early on in the design phase.

DESIGN CHOICES

Instead of big logs, natural touches such as pine trim, a reclaimed barnwood accent wall, and a decorative stack of "firewood" supporting the staircase convey a sense of the surroundings. "I didn't want the cliché rustic," says Paul. "This looks like what my house would look like in Chicago, but with a little more wood." Only, no Windy City skyline here—just Big Sky forests and rugged peaks as the breathtaking backdrop.

Back when Paul was contemplating a cabin, he knew it had to be in the Rockies. After looking at potential sites from Idaho to New Mexico, he wound up back in this corner of a state he

"OUT HERE IN THIS PART OF THE COUNTRY, THERE'S SO MUCH TO TAKE IN."

The upstairs workstation hosts a desk, chair, and bookshelf—no more, no less.

first visited at age six. "The Flathead Valley is really unique," he marvels. "You've got Kalispell, which is big enough to have all the stuff you need, but it's still kind of a cool little town. You've got the ski town of Whitefish, and then small tourist towns like Bigfork. And you've got plenty of locals mixing with people from all over the country." A patchwork of landownership provides access to Glacier National Park and other wild places. The area also offers ample opportunities to be in and on water, including Flathead Lake—the largest freshwater lake west of the Mississippi. Numerous rivers and creeks wend through the mountains that drew Paul in the first place.

"Out here in this part of the country, there's so much to take in," agrees Gerbozy. "So we decided it was important to build something based on Paul's needs and ensure the lot, the views, and the terrain fit those parameters." As a result, cabin windows were thoughtfully placed to maximize both view and light; a fabulous wraparound porch provides additional living space and an opportunity to survey the valley below.

PLAYTIME

The cabin has proved to be the perfect retreat for Paul and his canine pal. In fact, Ivan had a "paw" in the design considerations, making sure that no corner went unused. The otherwise empty space under the stairs was outfitted as a built-in doghouse—Ivan's favorite place to snooze after outings.

Given the countless year-round opportunities for adventure, Paul's response to another question about favorites—this time about activities in the region—is equally enthusiastic. "I like to hike, of course," he says. "And I do a little mountain biking. Really, you want to get involved in everything out here. Hiking in the winter is possible, and snowshoeing, and I do a little cross-country skiing. And stand-up paddleboarding in the summer. And I have a kayak . . ." ∎

By choosing a loft bedroom, Larson was able to maximize his use of space and create a bright, cozy haven.

This cottage has extraordinary charm, largely due to the details.

THINK SMALL

It's not the size of a home or cabin that counts; what matters is how well it suits the lifestyle of its occupants. That's the basic premise of respected architect Sarah Susanka, author of the ground-breaking book *The Not So Big House: A Blueprint for the Way We Really Live*. In a nutshell, Susanka advocates approaching the design of a home in a thoughtful, honest manner by asking yourself what is necessary and important in order to live comfortably, in an environment that is life-enhancing?

Rebbecca Abair has the answer figured out. Several years ago, she decided to build a timber-frame cottage on a slice of Puget Sound ground she had acquired near Port Orchard, Washington. "She sure knew what she was after," recalls Kelvin Mooney of the British Columbia Timberframe Company (BCTC) in Squamish, British Columbia. "She wanted a small house, in part due to the constraints of her waterfront parcel." The lot was narrow—just sixty feet wide— and 160 feet deep, and Puget Sound building setbacks are considerable due to environmental regulations. "Budget was also a consideration for choosing to build small," Mooney continues. "But primarily, Rebbecca was simply most happy living in cozy spaces."

This Pacific Coast cottage delivers proof that good things come in small packages.

"Unfitted pieces" were all part of the owner's kitchen design.

Not only did Rebbecca prefer to dwell in small homes, she had a passion for building them. She explained to Mooney up front that she intended to be her own general contractor (she had already built five homes for herself), and that he would need to agree to her hands-on involvement in the project, including the erection of the timber frame. A small-house enthusiast himself, Mooney was excited to be a part of Rebbecca's team.

THE DESIGN PROCESS

The design of the 1,155-square-foot cottage was driven by Rebbecca, and BCTC's in-house architect drew the final engineered plans. The location's breathtaking scenery dictated that the primary living areas face the water. Rebbecca laid out a floor plan that placed her sunroom and dining area at the rear of the house, with expansive views of the beach and water.

The kitchen and living room were positioned on the cottage's front-entry side, and a half bath was situated in the center of the main floor

The living room has a fireplace for cool evenings.

Outside, cedar shakes and a vintage hickory rocker give a rustic feel.

In the cottage's bathroom, a vintage claw-foot tub and side table are just a couple of the owner's found treasures.

DESIGN CONSIDERATIONS FOR SMALL COTTAGES

Small cottages and cabins offer housing that is more affordable to acquire, easier to maintain, and more ecologically friendly. Here are some aspects of small-house design to consider:

- **In addition to costing less, small houses may encourage a less cluttered environment and simpler lifestyle.**
- **Small houses typically emphasize function over size, and incorporate technological advances of space-saving equipment and appliances.**
- **A full basement foundation and second story are inexpensive ways to increase living space within a compact footprint.**
- **Porches, decks, and patios help a small house to live larger. The outdoor living season can be extended with the use of screening, an outdoor fireplace, or a simple fire pit.**
- **Landscaping is best kept natural, so that the home blends with the environment, softening the transition between natural surroundings and dwelling.**
- **Reclaimed materials go a long way in a small house. In addition to the economical reward of using reclaimed materials, there is the bonus of knowing that a home is unique and special.**

"THERE IS SO MUCH MORE TO LIFE THAN TAKING CARE OF STUFF THAT YOU DON'T NEED."

beneath the stairs. The living room flows into the sunroom, where east-facing double-hung windows welcome the morning sun.

The simple, craftsman-style staircase ascends from the foyer to a partial second level with a bedroom, a full bath, and a utility closet housing a stackable washer and dryer.

In the cottage's bathroom, a vintage claw-foot tub and side table are just a couple of Rebbecca's "found treasures." Others are part of her kitchen: the sink was found in a field, scraped clean, and repainted. And the antique worktable once belonged to a clock repairman.

The cottage is "a perfect design solution for a single person, or even a couple," says Mooney. "We have produced this timber-frame package for numerous clients since building Rebbecca's and have developed expanded versions of it as well, which provide a second bedroom in a walk-out basement. The footprint remains the same, but another full story is gained."

Facing east overlooking Puget Sound, the deck is the perfect perch for a morning cup of coffee.

OUTDOOR LIVING

The sunroom opens out onto a cedar deck—the optimal coastal pleasure. Facing east overlooking Puget Sound, it's the perfect perch for a morning cup of coffee. The railings are anchored to staunch posts faced with Eldorado manufactured stone. Cedar shakes and a vintage hickory rocker give it a rustic feel.

IT TAKES A SPECIAL PERSON

Since building her waterfront cottage, Rebbecca Abair has moved on to new small-house projects. "I found myself using very little of the cottage space and wanted to take the smaller home concept even further," she says. "I bought another piece of property and have designed a small cabin large enough to house only the things that make me smile, that I truly love, and have a connection to."

Rebbecca's design process includes many hours of sketching multipurpose built-ins and custom cabinetry to fit the tiny space, which is 230 square feet on the main floor with a 130-square-foot sleeping loft, accessed by a custom "Rebbecca-built ladder," for a total of 360 square feet. Meanwhile, she is living in a 200-square-foot cabin (yes . . . she built this one also) on the same property, originally intended to be a storage shed.

"It takes a special person to live in a tiny space," Rebbecca admits. "Most people think I'm crazy . . . or brilliant! I got kind of carried away with the shed and now it has a small kitchenette, a wood-burning cookstove, a custom-built cabinet/ desk, and a toilet room. I love living small! There is so much more to life than taking care of stuff that you don't need, certainly not in order to be happy." ■

The living room flows into the sunroom, where east-facing windows welcome the morning sun into the cottage.

THE REMODELED CABIN

The cabins in this section have been remodeled, renovated, or added on to. The cabin owners' motivations range widely. Some bravely and passionately seek to save a decrepit retreat from the wrecking ball, while others want to remake a cabin so that it's their own, and some just want to freshen up their cottage with a facelift. Regardless, all of the projects are inspiring and full of ideas.

The owners of this 1920s cabin were going to raze it and start over, but they opted for a strip-to-the-studs rebuild instead.

"THE CABIN IS PART OF OUR LEGACY—ONE THAT OUR KIDS AND GRANDKIDS CAN ENJOY FOR YEARS TO COME."

A COMFY NORTHWOODS GETAWAY

Mike Jacob was in middle school when his parents bought a seasonal retreat on Minnesota's Girl Lake, located 175 miles north of the Twin Cities. Mike and his siblings adored spending summers at the cabin, but once they started broods of their own, it grew crowded.

Mike and his wife, Dana, began hunting for a place of their own and stumbled upon a rustic 1920s hunting shack on Woman Lake, just seven miles from his parents' place. Before the realtor showed the property, he warned the Jacobs, "Now remember, you're buying *shoreline*."

"We stepped inside and could literally see the 2 x 4s that made the interior walls and the half-log that made the exterior," recalls Dana.

The floors were covered in dirty linoleum. The exposed electrical system ran on fuses. With no stove, cooking was done with plug-in burners. The makeshift shower consisted of a tin bucket suspended on a string by a pulley system.

Having to work with the original footprint forced the Jacobs to keep things small and cozy.

The shoreline was obstructed by overgrown brush. But that shoreline was only forty feet from the cabin— a huge plus. The Jacobs also loved the fieldstone fireplace in the middle of the room.

They promptly made an offer and began researching ways to transform the cabin into a nicer living space while preserving its vintage Northwoods charm.

NO-GO ON THE BULLDOZE

Over the next ten years, Mike and Dana met with several builders. Each suggested bulldozing the place and starting from scratch. The problem was, building regulations required new construction to be set back seventy-five feet from the water.

In one of the bathrooms, a family sewing table serves as a washstand. The mirror was fashioned from an old window.

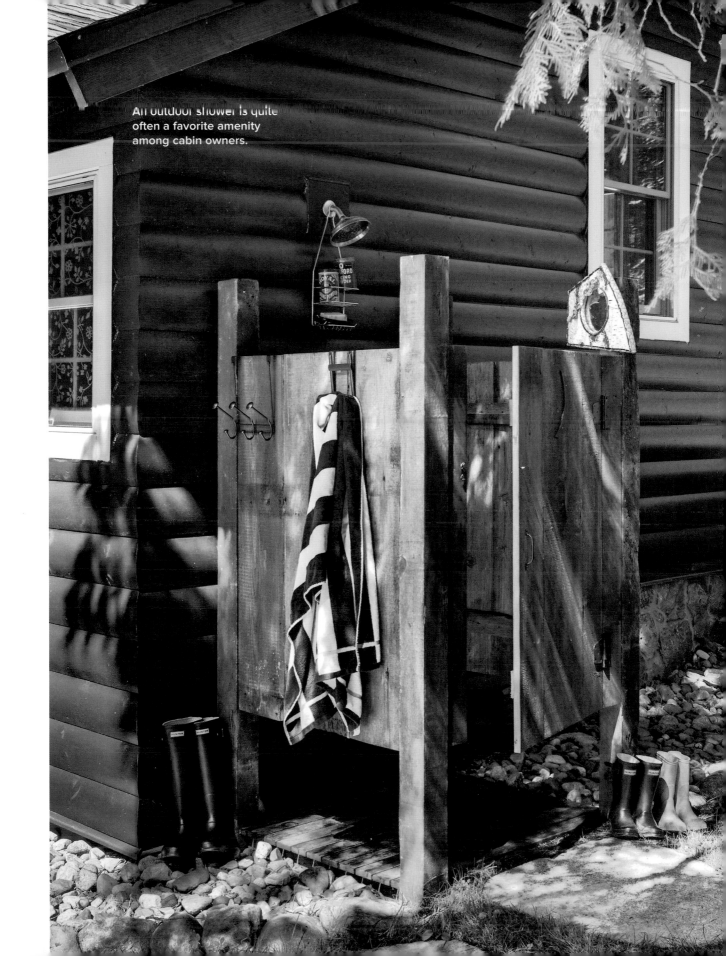

An outdoor shower is quite
often a favorite amenity
among cabin owners.

The built-in beds in the hallways were designed for guest use but are also quiet nooks for reading.

The Jacobs wanted to stay put. Besides, they'd grown fond of their eclectic quarters. Then the couple met with brothers Jeff and Matt Balmer, owners of Lands End Development in Crosslake, Minnesota. Mike and Dana explained that they wanted to keep the "bare walls look" and also do something with the old windows. Most importantly, they wanted the new place to still feel old.

Immediately, these fourth-generation builders got it. "All the other builders wanted *us* to get on board with *their* thinking," says Dana. "But Matt and Jeff listened to what we wanted and then came up with ways to make our dream a reality."

STICKING TO THE VISION

The Balmer building team knows how easy it is for cabin owners to get so carried away with the excitement of new construction that they lose sight of their original vision. "When you don't have limitations, you're tempted to keep adding space," says Jeff. "I've heard customers say, 'Oh, I'd love a couple more feet in the bedroom,' or 'Gee,

"YOU CAN'T GATHER FAMILY AROUND YOUR 401(K)."

honey, if we're going to retire up here, maybe we should do that attached garage.' It's a slippery slope," he warns.

In this case, zoning restrictions for the lake property prevented the addition of anything that didn't align with the initial goal. "[Working with the same footprint,] we were forced into that cozier feel," explains Jeff. "The small size and limitations is what created such a cool spot."

NEW PLACE, OLD FEEL

From an architectural standpoint, deliberate choices were made to attain an aged flavor, starting with preserving the original full-masonry fireplace. In addition, Jeff suggested rough-sawn beams and lower wall heights (seven and a half feet vs. nine). He also recommended simple roof lines and smaller, mullioned windows, along with a limited use of drywall. Exposed rafter tails at the overhangs and varied (as opposed to matching) header heights enhance the old-fashioned appearance. Stone veneer covering the concrete block simulates an old stone foundation.

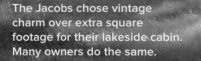

The Jacobs chose vintage charm over extra square footage for their lakeside cabin. Many owners do the same.

Window treatments, as well as vintage furniture, can add homey touches to a room.

Interior choices such as reclaimed flooring, glazed cabinets, vintage appliances, and antique furnishings all contributed to the timeworn look. Interior designer Michelle Fries worked with the owners to create a space that felt cozy, comfy, and undeniably cabin. "I grew up spending summers at seasonal cabins," says Michelle. "They were tiny and drafty and had mismatched sheets, dishes, and appliances." Simplicity ruled.

FAVORITE PLACES AND SPACES

The Jacobs, too, love simple spaces such as the built-in beds in the hallway. When it's snowing or overcast outside, Dana climbs into one, closes the curtain, and snuggles up with a book. "Occasionally, I'll have to remind Dana that she can sleep with me in the bedroom," Mike says with a chuckle. "I tell her, 'I promise I showered today!'"

And chances are, he did so in his favorite cabin amenity—the outdoor shower. Mike says he enjoys the outdoor facilities so much that he refuses to clean up indoors between March and October.

During the mild months, the couple regularly uses the covered back porch, which they refer to as the "Minnesota Room." Mike says, "It expands our living area, particularly when the wind is coming off the water and it's too cold to sit lakeside."

A JOY FOR EVERY SEASON

In the fall, Mike takes his black Labrador retriever duck hunting. Dana appreciates autumn's vibrant landscape, but says the gold and red leaves signal that temps will soon plunge.

When Jack Frost comes a-nippin', the couple bundles up and glides across the area's groomed cross-country trails. They are also eager to test their snowmobiles and give ice fishing a try. (They recently purchased an ice-fishing shelter, which will double as overflow guest quarters in the summer.)

Summertime is, by far, the couple's favorite season. They spend hours playing on and in the water. Often, the Jacobs zip over to Girl Lake on their pontoon boat to

The Jacobs decorated their cabin with native and reclaimed materials and scaled the furniture to fit the room.

join Mike's clan (just ten minutes away by boat). Or the families bring portable grills and gather on the sandbar to play Frisbee, water volleyball, baseball, and football. Sometimes they play the game Catch Phrase with Mike's folks.

Dana and Mike also own a Chris-Craft, which they take out on clear nights—along with a bottle of wine—to watch the sun set.

Each year, the couple hosts a Fourth of July bash. Their three grown children, along with dozens of aunts, uncles, cousins, and kiddos, come together to eat hearty, laugh plenty, and make wonderful memories. There's always a huge bonfire, tons of barbeque, and, of course, the highly anticipated beanbag tourney.

The Jacobs knew from the get-go that the cabin was the perfect place for family gatherings.

"When we bought the place, I remember saying to Dana, 'This is a great investment because you can't gather family around your 401(k),' " recalls Mike. "The cabin is part of our legacy—one that our kids and grandkids can enjoy for years to come." ■

A small cottage on the surf side of Nantucket Island is ideal for a summer escape, especially if it has great outdoor living spaces.

SURFSIDE COTTAGE

Renovating a cottage for someone in the hospitality industry, who knows the myriad details that go into making people comfortable, might give an architect pause. But Lisa Botticelli of Botticelli & Pohl Architects in Nantucket had already designed one house for Herb Rose and his wife, Anne, an artist. She knew the three shared a similar vision: an appreciation for simple things done well.

For years, Anne and the couple's three boys summered in their four-bedroom vacation home in Nantucket (in town), with Herb joining them on weekends from their primary home in New York City. But once the Roses became empty nesters, they sought to downsize their retreat.

The couple found a classic beach cottage on the ocean side—the surf side—of the island. The traditional 1950s uninsulated, two-bedroom retreat rested on a part of Nantucket with wide-open land and plenty of sky. The Roses called on Botticelli to make it inviting year-round, while preserving the exposed beam interior and the brick fireplace in the master bedroom.

Extra-wide, low steps make the back lawn effortlessly accessible.

White walls and ceilings are found throughout the cottage. Wood floors instead of ceramic tile are cozier for bare feet.

SMALL DONE RIGHT

The project held great appeal for Lisa Botticelli.

"It's rare that you get to do a little building like this for owners interested in doing it well," Botticelli says. "With a building this small, you can think about every square inch."

The design had to pass muster with the Historic District Commission, which it did easily because the Roses stayed true to the original footprint. The couple was not interested in "making a statement" with the cottage, but they did want to be comfortable while enjoying its charm.

The Roses felt strongly about preserving the interior plank walls and exposed beams of rough-sawn lumber—i.e., wood that has not been planed and is thicker than conventional "dressed" boards. Thus, rigid insulation had to be layered on the exterior and resheathed, and then the wood-shingle siding had to be put back on. (Note: A new energy code put into effect in Massachusetts since that time no longer allows this technique, which only accommodates four inches of insulation.)

Natural materials factored into the renovation. Many homes today use medium-density

White and bright blues pair together nicely along with abundant windows and doors to get a beachy vibe.

The Roses' kitchen is small and practical. They often will take the food outside to grill on their large deck when family comes by.

Light-toned rugs hide sand trekked in from outside and pet hair from wet dogs.

fiberboard (MDF), an engineered product that can be grooved to mimic beadboard. It is installed in sheets that don't respond to moisture by expanding, contracting, or cracking the way wood does. Many people consider that an advantage, but the Roses wanted the home to age naturally, so they used only wood in the renovation.

"The home celebrates the use of materials," Botticelli says. She recommended fir for the floors, because it is a little soft underfoot. A high-gloss finish creates a polished modern look. For the interior trims and moldings, the architect chose poplar—a smooth, fine-grained wood that takes paint well.

The whole interior—walls, vaulted ceilings, exposed-brick fireplaces in the master bedroom and living room—was painted white. Cheerful blue fabrics and the Roses' blue bottle collection pair nicely with white for a beachy ambiance, while artwork throughout the cottage provides pops of color. The kitchen is pint-size and practical, just right for two. (The couple often takes food outside to grill when family comes by.) English-looking brass plumbing was selected to fit the down-to-earth style.

TRUE TO FORM

The Roses did not want the cottage to look brand-new when finished; rather, it should fit in with the other understated, mid-century beach homes on that part of the island. For the construction, the Roses hired a friend of the family.

"We joked that we wanted the builder to put his worst carpenter on this job," Botticelli says. "Seams that aren't perfect add to the flavor of the architecture. Finding a builder who gets what you're trying to do is key. You don't want it to look cacophonous, but to look like it has aged gracefully."

LESSONS IN RENOVATION

Here are some lessons homeowners might consider before taking on a historic home renovation:

- Look at the house objectively to see what of architectural merit should be saved. The hard truth is that sometimes it is most expedient and less expensive to tear down the original home and rebuild from scratch.
- Make sure you have a plan and a budget before the contractor lifts the first hammer.
- Finally, find out how much or even whether a home can be enlarged. Oftentimes, a historic home can't have additions.

Keep furniture simple at your getaway. Go for inviting and comfortable.

Herb is quick to credit Botticelli for appreciating the patina of age. "Lisa was very good at interpreting that popular cottage vernacular," he says. "When you look in the cottage, it's hard to believe that it is essentially a new house."

INSIDE AND OUTSIDE

The original cottage had a screen porch that the Roses converted to an uninsulated sunroom. They preserved the decking on the floor, then framed in large, screened windows that operate on pulleys to hinge open inside and hook to the ceiling. Depending

on the direction of the prevailing wind, they can close the windows on one side to deflect a strong breeze while still enjoying the sense of being outdoors and being protected from the elements.

Because the cottage is small, it draws natural light from multiple directions. The Roses underscored the natural light by replacing the standard-size front and back doors with extra-wide models. The sight line from the front door extends all the way through the house and out to the ocean.

OUTDOOR LIVING

How does a big family fit into a small vacation home? By living outdoors more than in.

Now that the Roses have retired, they spend the whole summer at their two-bedroom cottage in Nantucket. When their three grown sons—and their wives and children—come to visit, "they're obliged to rent their own places," Herb Rose says, "which isn't necessarily the worst thing."

When the entire clan gets together for the day and evening, they spread out across the huge deck that embraces two sides of the cottage. The expanse is broken up into outdoor "rooms"—distinct areas for grilling, dining, sunbathing, or sunset gatherings by the outdoor fireplace. (It backs up to the fireplace in the master bedroom.) Even better, one can see the ocean from the deck. Cottage-goers spill down three low steps onto the grassy lawn that extends to a beach pathway. The finished surfside cottage offers exactly what the Roses wanted: casual indoor/outdoor "hospitality" for themselves and their guests. ◼

"SEAMS THAT AREN'T PERFECT ADD TO THE FLAVOR OF THE ARCHITECTURE."

It took vision to breathe new life into this reclaimed ranch that's all about the guests.

"WE TRIED TO NOT TAKE
ANYTHING PAST WHAT IT USED
TO BE."

WELCOME BACK

When the new owners found it, the Colorado ranch house was sagging off a loose stone foundation. Most of the original flooring, installed when the ranch was built in the early 1900s, was gone. Doors were missing. Windows were broken. Trees had fallen on the roof, leaving sunlight streaming through the ceiling. Rodents had moved in. Delicately put, "it was in a difficult state," says Bill Coburn, owner of Coburn Development, Inc., and lead visionary on the restoration team that brought Coburn's newly acquired cabin back to life in 2001.

If the ranch's age was a liability to its last residents—a family of cattle ranchers who moved out in the 1960s—it would become the building's lifeline to rescuers Coburn and team. The crew cut their teeth renovating structures that were just as dilapidated in Boulder, Colorado. "Our background was having the vision to look at something in that incredible state of disrepair and see a way to make it work," says Coburn. He was intent on preserving the building's history. And since it's nestled in a picturesque spot right next to the river on the 300-acre Gunnison River Ranch development

A snapshot of the original cabin shows its sagging foundation, missing windows, and warped siding. But the idyllic setting made the revamp worthwhile.

The ranch's outdoor sink is handy for cleaning boots, gear, or fish.

near the town of Gunnison, he knew the old place would make an ideal guesthouse and fly-fishing hub for the development's residents.

LIKE STEPPING BACK IN TIME

Fun amenities, a clubhouse feel for fly-fishermen, and historic preservation were high on the list of priorities for the renovation. Not only would the ranch be a place where guests could unwind, have fun with friends, and prep fishing gear, the experience would be like stepping back in time. Old barns, fence posts, outhouses, ranching implements—even a retired railroad bridge over the river—are scattered throughout the acreage surrounding the ranch house. "We fixed everything up to a certain level where it would sustain itself, but we tried to not take anything past what it used to be," he says.

As much as possible, updates to the 1,100-square-foot ranch house, which includes a great room, two bedrooms, two bathrooms, and a laundry room, followed the same idea. Initially, the team talked about expanding the guesthouse's footprint or adding a second story. But, Coburn says, the ranch's spot on the river made it "really sweet and quaint," and the team ultimately decided against a major addition. "It would've been a disservice to try to make the ranch house more than it was—it would've been changing its feel," he says.

ONE STRATEGIC ADDITION

For starters, the team raised the structure to install a pressure-treated wood foundation that would hold up to the area's fairly wet conditions. After getting the ranch back on solid footing, they made one strategic addition: a wraparound porch. Not only does this outdoor living space invite relaxation, it helps keep the ranch cool and offers

A spacious wraparound porch and a substantial outdoor fireplace offer guests a relaxing space.

A pair of twin beds makes this room the "bachelor pad," jokes the owner.

Guests in the restored ranch enjoy fly-fishing in the Gunnison River, which flows right outside.

a prep area for fly-fishermen. Coburn, an avid fly-fisherman himself, says the ranch is "all set up for showing up and preparing to go fish and then lightly entertaining before, during, and after."

The porch's outdoor fireplace and tin roof are ideal for entertaining. "You can look up and actually see the tin," says Coburn. "So it's really nice when you stand out there and it's raining and you get that little pitter-patter; that's by design." A nearby cookhouse offers a smoker and charcoal and gas grills. Guests can also enjoy a fire pit or play horseshoes. The team relocated an old cabin to the area and converted it into a game house with darts, foosball, table tennis, and poker and pool tables. Coburn says the options are intentional; one of the ways the team likes to create spaces that feel good is to include a series of places for people to hang out. Exterior posts and columns, as well as the cookhouse and a footbridge, are all indigenous Douglas fir pieces, reclaimed from a cattle stockyard in Pueblo, Colorado.

SOLUTIONS THAT ADD CHARACTER

The interior of the ranch house owes much of its rich character to what Coburn says was the team's most controversial decision. Coburn wanted to keep the original interior walls, so the 2 x 4s would remain exposed. To do this, they used 2 x 6s to build a shell around the exterior, and ran plumbing, wiring, and insulation between the layers. Lap cedar siding was added to the new exterior framing. To maintain most of the original ceilings, the team used a similar technique; they removed the original roof and overframed the existing ceilings with 2 x 10 joists, then tucked insulation in between.

In the great room, Coburn says, they did some "selective truss work" to vault the ceiling over the living, dining, and kitchen areas. The ceiling now

"IT'S SUPPOSED TO LOOK LIKE A HORSE SOMEHOW WALKED THROUGH THE HOUSE AND LEFT ITS MARK."

stands fifteen feet tall. Collar ties had been holding the original roof-framing together. For the vault upgrade, Coburn wanted to forgo very large timbers; instead, iron tie beams make the trusses more airy. "We don't have a ton of volume and we don't have a ton of space," says Coburn of the 25 x 18-foot room. "We wanted to create trusses that weren't overbearing, so what you're really experiencing is just the volume."

The centerpiece of the great room is the corner fireplace, which stands back-to-back with the outdoor fireplace on the porch. The two have individual fireboxes and chimneys, but appear joined. Neither fireplace is original to the ranch, though the red sandstone cobbles look like they could have been gathered from the river right outside the door. When there's no fire roaring, a forced-air furnace keeps the ranch cozy.

To admit more light, new windows were cut into walls; some were positioned in enlarged openings at original locations. Wherever walls and ceilings couldn't be preserved, new lumber was added and whitewashed to maintain the rustic feel while brightening up the spaces.

The ranch's flooring was not salvageable, so the team laid a new manufactured pine floor, then distressed it with chains and bags of rocks. "When you walk into this building, you have all these old walls. The material's very tactile . . . it just feels and

The ranch house is stocked with extra fishing gear in case guests forget anything.

Built from reclaimed wood beams during the renovation, the bunks offer guests semi-private sleeping nooks with built-in reading lights.

HOW TO MAKE YOUR CABIN ANGLER-FRIENDLY

A large wraparound porch offers anglers a sheltered place to sort their gear, get ready, and rig their rods before heading to the river. An outdoor sink is handy for cleaning boots, gear, or fish, and a dog-wash area is great for bathing your dog before it hops back in the car. It also works for cleaning muddy boots or coolers. Having all of these amenities outside means the mess stays outside.

Stock extra gear in case guests forget anything. Keep on hand extra flies, wading boots, and fishing rods.

If you're not into fishing but your guests are, visit your local fishing shops to get the best recommendations for where your guests can get their waders wet.

looks super vintage and rustic, so we didn't want a big new shiny floor to dominate the room," says Coburn. While craftsmen "blind-nailed" the floor to hide the nails, they also drove in square-head nails for an aged look. And in keeping with the ranch theme, they even branded the floor with a horseshoe in select areas. "You really would have to look hard to realize that it's supposed to look like a horse somehow walked through the house and left its mark," says Coburn. "It was a fun little goofy addition."

EVOCATIVE DECORATING CHOICES

Coburn and his wife, Annie, spearheaded the interior design. Annie selected the couch to fit her vision of the guesthouse as a "gentleman rancher's retreat." The warm leather evokes the Old West, but its lines are soft— an important consideration, since the guesthouse is used by both men and women.

Annie intentionally chose a set of chairs that weren't made for the trestle-style dining table. When pieces look as though they've been gathered over the years, she explains, it lends a sense of historic authenticity. Several reclaimed pieces in the great room also elicit that sense of history: the rusted metal partition wall between dining and kitchen areas, the solid coffee table made of vintage wood, and the standing lamp made of a retrofitted surveyor's tripod. The large brown trout mounted on the fireplace is a wood carving by a local artist. Aside from sconces in the bedrooms, the Coburns de-emphasized the lighting by hiding small monopoint fixtures in the ceiling.

All this attention to detail has made the guesthouse a favorite place for entertaining and relaxing. Coburn says visitors often reserve it for dinner parties, cookouts, and, of course, fly-fishing trips. The surrounding land still operates as a cattle ranch. Given the work that Coburn and his team have already put into the place, let's hope the steers don't develop a hankerin' to play foosball. ■

Winter at this Montana cabin means cross-country skiing and quiet weekends around the woodstove.

"THERE WAS SOMETHING ABOUT IT—MAYBE THE WRAPAROUND PORCH—THAT FELT LIKE HOME AS SOON AS I TOURED IT."

DIY CABIN REMODEL

In the beginning, the outlook wasn't entirely rosy at the little farmhouse in Bigfork, Montana. "There were definitely times, initially, that we thought we had bought a lemon," says Felesha McAfee.

Felesha recalls the winter when she and husband Jeremiah began renovating the farmhouse they had just purchased. "The day we got the keys, we started tearing the ceiling out. That was the beginning of a year and a half of work."

A MAMMOTH REMODEL

Although eager, neither had ever renovated a cabin—nor any kind of home, for that matter. They soon learned that the process entailed more than a few challenges. "We gutted the house, and then even gutted the guts!" Felesha recalls. "Every time we pulled down a wall, we discovered another problem behind that problem." They ended up replacing all of the house's innards, including wiring and plumbing. They also reconfigured floor plans, moved walls, cut doors, added bathrooms, demolished the kitchen, and other Herculean tasks.

The owners saw their outdated farmhouse as a blank slate, ready to be tailored to their precise needs and wants.

The end result of the remodel is a cozy picture-perfect retreat.

Felesha admits that she's not sure what first attracted her to the cabin, given its unpromising appearance. Built in 1920, the place had been remodeled in the '70s and it showed—from the wood paneling to the garish wallpaper to the turquoise tub. Yet the fact that it wasn't a traditional Montana cabin resonated with this Ohio native. "There was something about it—maybe the wraparound porch—that felt like home as soon as I toured it," Felesha recalls. Maybe this was a place where she and Jeremiah could live full-time at some point, with room for additional family as well.

LABOR OF LOVE

Despite early misgivings, the McAfees stuck with the project. A year and a half later, their sweat equity paid off. The result is a two-bedroom, two-bath cabin as charming as it is comfortable.

The aesthetic is a perfect blend of midwestern farmhouse and western rustic. Wide floorboards pair nicely with new shiplap paneling throughout much of cabin. White floors, walls, and ceilings reflect the light, brightening what was once a dimly lit space. A reclaimed tin ceiling in the kitchen highlights the same earth tones as the new tiled backsplash. An old ladder, festooned with lights, hangs above a doorway. The built-in cupboard with screen doors is a nod to the pie safe of a bygone era. Understated beams and reclaimed barnwood lend an air of history and warmth.

SOURCING THE GOODS

"We were lucky enough that Jeremiah was able to barter labor for materials with a company here that salvages old grain elevators and barns," says Felesha, referring to Wild Wood Eccentrics, a reclaimed wood business based in Columbia Falls, Montana. "He'd work all day, then go and work more for them," she recalls. "All that material became our trim, our floors, our barn doors."

With an eye toward maintaining an authentic, rustic feel, Felesha combed antique stores and Craigslist for furnishings and finishing touches. One old cabinet was repurposed as a vanity. Other accessories came from consignment shops or from family in Ohio. Her favorite find is the cast-iron pedestal tub that plays a starring role in the spacious first-floor bathroom. "It's so beautiful, and we only paid a few hundred bucks. It came out of an old home in Kalispell, which I love—from one farmhouse

The owners opened up their living space by removing walls and a chimney and raising the ceiling.

5 TIPS FOR WORKING WITH BARNWOOD

Reclaimed barnwood is a favored material of designers these days. While it lends a charming, rustic feel to any room, it can be problematic to work with. Old lumber can be warped, checked, brittle, dirty and just plain fickle.

Builders and woodworkers have a number of tips for working with this tricky material:

1. **Some of the reclaimed wood you purchased won't be useable, so buy a bit more than you'll need.**

2. **When it comes to old, painted wood, it's best to assume that any paint is lead-based. Saw off and discard the painted wood or coat it in a high-quality polyurethane to seal it. First be sure to remove all old nails, for the safety of both you and your tools.**

3. **If boards are especially dirty—such as floorboards from an old barn—a stout wire brush will enable you to remove a large majority of the dirt without impacting the patina.**

4. **Planing one side of the board flat will make it easier to affix to a wall or include in a piece of furniture, without losing any of the character of the un-planed side.**

5. **Most importantly, be comfortable with the quirks, character, and oddities that barnwood will bring to your project. After all, that's why you chose it in the first place!**

Love at first sight: The new owners of this cabin fell in love with the wraparound porch when they first toured the property.

Barnwood lends a charming, rustic feel to any room, but it can be tricky to work with.

to another," Felesha remembers. Re-enameled and fitted with antique-style hardware, the tub is flanked by windows—a perfect vantage point for watching the snow fall in winter.

FUN ON FLATHEAD

By mid-2015, "Swan River Farmhouse" was ready for guests other than the McAfees themselves. "The intent was always to rent it out in the summer, at least initially," says Felesha. Located on the northern end of Flathead Lake, Bigfork is a bustling tourist town in the warmer months. Vacationers come from around the state and beyond to enjoy both water activities and the area's myriad cultural amenities. But Felesha doesn't really mind missing out on summer. "I love how quiet and sleepy the town gets in the off-season. Winter is our time, and we get to come down to hang out, go cross-country skiing with our dogs, and work on projects to get the place ready for summer again." Because the couple lives in nearby Whitefish, the trip to the cabin is an easy jaunt for a weekend getaway but far enough to feel like a true vacation home.

White floors, walls, and ceiling reflect the light, brightening what was once a dimly lit space.

Open shelving, a barnwood ceiling, a deep sink, and antique accents in the kitchen reference the home's history as a farmhouse.

NO REGRETS

The McAfees will be the first to admit that renovating a house down to the studs (and beyond) is a daunting experience to tackle alone, especially without prior experience. And yet, when asked if they would do it again, Felesha doesn't miss a beat: "Yes, we would." Then she pauses a moment to reflect. "Okay, I would definitely do the 'lipstick and rouge' part of it again" she laughs. "Maybe not quite everything that we did!" ■

Doing it himself, one man transforms a hunter's cabin into a personal getaway.

CABIN IN THE HILLS

Sometimes, the seed of an idea takes years—even decades—to germinate and come to fruition. But so often, it's these slow-growing dreams that are most worth the wait. Such was the case with Mehosh Dziadzio's rebuilt cabin in southern California's Los Padres National Forest.

"As a child growing up on my grandparents' farm in upstate New York, I watched my grandfather, a Polish immigrant after whom I was named, take a run-down farmhouse built in the 1850s and transform it into something beautiful," says Mehosh. "That's what inspired me to one day do that myself."

CAPTURING A DREAM

As the youngster grew into an adult, Mehosh gathered the skills necessary to one day turn that childhood vision into a reality. Over the years, he was employed as an electrician's assistant and lived for seven years on a commune where he learned to work with his hands. Eventually, Mehosh became a self-taught professional photographer with an eye for beauty and detail. Mehosh's photography career took off in the late 1980s, and he found himself living and working in his Santa Barbara

Native American artwork can be found gracing the walls of this rustic retreat. Rugs, throws, and curtains add to the overall feeling.

studio. In search of a retreat, he stumbled upon a ramshackle, Depression-era hunting cabin twenty miles outside of the city.

"It was in bad shape," Mehosh recalls, "which enabled me to pick it up pretty cheaply. My original intent was to fix it up and have a weekend getaway, but I quickly discovered that it would be easier starting from scratch rather than building on what was already there."

And thus, years of planning, saving, scavenging, and creating began. Mehosh soon realized that only the floor and rustic stone fireplace were salvageable. He began designing a new cabin that would be based on the original cabin's footprint but would incorporate elements that were meaningful to him. "I'd always been drawn to the rustic

Visitors enjoy restful nights in this spacious room.

Native American elements and
Southwestern décor are used
even in the bathroom.

A kitchen doesn't have to be large to fit everything in, just practical.

This bedroom features exposed logs.

vacation resorts along the Hudson River, which gained popularity in the late 1800s," Mehosh recalls. "Other influences were the houses I saw in my travels throughout the Southwest, which used natural elements of earth, wood, and plaster to create an organic feel. My challenge was how to incorporate the two."

INSPIRED DESIGN

With this vision in mind—and holding tight to his lifelong dream of building a place entirely on his own—Mehosh set to work. "Using the existing floor plan, I put pencil to paper and drafted a set of plans in a matter of weeks," he says. "Room by room,

"I'M ONLY THIRTY MINUTES FROM TOWN, BUT IT FEELS LIKE I'M FAR FROM CIVILIZATION."

I envisioned what it should look like. Not having a comprehensive understanding of county codes or structural requirements, I took my drawings to an architectural designer, who drafted a set of plans I could deliver to the building department for permits."

Ultimately, Mehosh created a design that reflects East Coast and Adirondack styles on the exterior, with Southwestern elements. Plans in hand, he then faced the next major hurdle: making those plans a reality. "At first, I questioned if I could pull this off," says Mehosh. "Even my closest friends thought I was crazy, but I was determined to do this. I had no formal training in construction, but I was able to pick it up pretty quickly. Working with my hands and figuring things out as I go is something that has always come relatively easy to me."

Realizing only the floor and the fireplace were worth saving was one of the owner's biggest challenges.

The interior is warm and inviting, exquisitely decorated with Native American art, Southwest-style furnishings, and rich earth tones.

THE RIGHT MATERIALS

Having sunk his savings into the property, Mehosh was faced with the additional challenge of procuring building materials. In the early 1990s, the "reclaimed materials" aesthetic was not extremely popular. But, with an eye toward thriftiness—and ecological integrity—Mehosh began amassing unwanted and unused lumber, hardware, furniture, and more. In fact, he spent several years just collecting materials before he began construction.

"I needed to save where I could if I was going to complete this project in a timely manner," says Mehosh. "And being familiar with people in the trades, I was tipped off when a demolition was about to happen. I'd go to the job site and load materials up in my van, whether I knew or not if they'd end up actually being used in the construction of my cabin. I knew that to be of clear conscience I would need to do my part and use recycled materials wherever I could."

THE PERFECT ESCAPE

Eventually, with a lot of hard work and assistance of friends, Mehosh's dream retreat took shape. Ten years after he purchased the property, the project was finally done. Low-slung and wood-sided, the cabin nestles into the hillside, surrounded by mature trees, simple landscaping, and native plants. Warm and inviting, the interior is exquisitely decorated with Native American art, Southwestern-style furnishings, and rich earth tones. Paneling and plaster bestow a natural, rustic feel, and windows provide gorgeous views of the surrounding forest.

Today, Mehosh uses the space just as he originally intended: as an escape from his hectic, on-the-go lifestyle. With nearly 3,000 square miles of national forest on the doorstep, opportunities to commune with nature are virtually unlimited. Hundreds of miles of hiking trails traverse Los Padres, rising from sea level to nearly 9,000 feet in elevation. When the mood strikes, Mehosh can work in the digital photography studio he built in the basement or party with neighbors. The location is ideal: As a professional photographer, he has easy access to the city and his work. But when it comes time to relax, Mehosh need only drive up the mountain to find himself in the heart of the wilderness.

"It's perfect. I'm surrounded by national forest and have deer that come right up to the deck in the mornings. I'm only thirty minutes from town, but it feels like I'm far from civilization. All of my friends comment on how peaceful it is," Mehosh says. "Traveling as much as I do, I never tire of coming home to my cabin in the woods." ■

Inside and out, this renovation is all about connecting with nature.

A RUSTIC CABIN GETS A DRAMATIC UPDATE

The moment that San Francisco natives Josh Feldman and Britton Watkins toured a woodland property for sale near Santa Rosa, they knew they need not look further. The 964-square-foot rustic retreat nestled amid nature's splendor. Surrounded by old-growth trees beside the soothing trickle of Mark West Creek, the place seemed as though it were deep within the forest, despite being surrounded by the Northern California wine country. (Sonoma Valley is directly south, Napa is just east, and the Russian River is to the west.)

Only sixty miles from San Francisco, the location was ideal for a weekend getaway.

There was just one problem. The 1930s cabin was erected in an era when structures were built solely for utilitarian purposes—in this instance, as a cooking cabin for the property owners who used their land for camping. As a result, "the cabin lacked connectivity to the creek," explains Britton. "If you were doing anything other than standing at the sink washing dishes, you couldn't see the creek."

This revamped creekside cabin is just what the owners wanted—an intimate sanctuary.

Situated in the heart of California wine country, the cabin is only sixty miles from San Francisco.

A FRESH FACE FOR THE SAME SPACE

Although Josh and Britton were eager to remodel in a way that would invite the outdoors in, they resisted any radical renovation measures. Instead, they opted to tackle the project in two phases.

Phase one involved unifying the structure by laying down the same engineered hardwood flooring throughout. Over the years, various owners had added on rooms and flooring in a piecemeal fashion, so that by the time Josh and Britton bought it in 2007, it was a "hodgepodge of Frankenstein additions: pine, plywood, cement, Mexican tile," says Britton.

Certain rooms required extra attention. In the kitchen, they retrofitted the cabinets with soft-closing drawers and cheery yellow paint, installed new hardware, and purchased a new dishwasher and sink. The master bath was refreshed with new cabinets and countertops, as well as new sinks, faucets, and tiling. The shower was updated with new glass and a teak floor with benches. The owners also added a wall to the upstairs loft and converted it into the master bedroom.

Limited storage space prompted Josh and Britton to design and install cabinets beneath the formerly open stairs. Inspired by traditional Japanese step tansu (staircase chest furniture), the units sport modern drawer mechanisms.

Finally, the couple installed a programmable thermostat. "We used to spend an hour dealing with the woodstove and ashes," notes Josh. "It was lots of work to just get to the point of being able to relax. Now on chilly days, we call the house to turn on the furnace before we arrive."

A ROOM WITH A VIEW

Phase two was all about creating a room with a view of the creek while preserving the integrity of

This new hallway, running along the outside of the original cabin, shows how the architect's renovation design married old and new.

The renovation increased storage space, including the step-tansu-inspired staircase cabinets and drawers.

More storage was added to the kitchen as well.

the original structure. The addition was conceived as a glass box wrapping the existing shingle-style cabin.

Renovating so close to the stream challenged Sonoma architect Amy Alper to determine the best way to support the new living room and hallway addition. The addition roughly follows the outline of an underutilized exterior deck that had to be removed. Structural steel beams and posts, set at deck support locations, carry a cantilevered floor, achieving maximum allowable new square footage with no added site disturbance.

The dismantled redwood deck members were reused onsite to enhance the connection between old and new.

"NOW ON CHILLY DAYS, WE CALL THE HOUSE TO TURN ON THE FURNACE BEFORE WE ARRIVE."

"With steel, we were able to cantilever the addition to reach the maximum allowed square footage and to set the new steel posts at only the points where the old [beetle-damaged] deck was supported by wood posts," explains Alper, who collaborated with a structural engineer on the project.

The dismantled redwood deck members were reused onsite, as were two period windows, to enhance the connection between old and new.

Because Britton had lived in Japan for a number of years, he asked Alper to incorporate an engawa in planning the hallway leading to the new addition. (An "engawa" is an external floor extension on Japanese houses that serves as a walkway.) "I wanted to infuse the quaint atmosphere of the old Japanese dwellings," explains Britton. Alper was happy to do so. In fact, she found the design of the addition to be a fun blend of past and present, historic and modern.

The bathroom reflects a Japanese influence.

Prior to the renovation, the creek could only be seen from the kitchen sink. The addition changed all that.

The owners also added to the new "old" look of the cabin by way of reclaimed wood. For instance, all of the wood used for the living room's beams came from dismantled structures in Sonoma County. A custom desk is also made out of salvaged wood with a natural "live edge" triangular slab top designed to fit perfectly into the new living room next to the sofa.

Although the desk is used as a workspace, it also hides electronics and cords for the room (Blu-ray player, stereo, etc.). And the reclaimed beams, which were installed at ten feet to make the room feel more intimate, hide speakers and wiring. "You don't see any modern technology screaming out at you," says Josh.

"It's about the marriage of old and new, context and contrast," says Alper. "By encasing the new living room—and new hallway connecting old to new—in glass, the cabin became open to the views of the creek and the steep forested hillside beyond."

The new design keeps the indoor temperature comfortable. The summer sun is mitigated by the dense forestation. In the winter, with less foliage, the lower-angled sun warms up the living area through the glass. The couple did not install air-conditioning since there are typically only a handful of days each year when temps exceed ninety degrees. On those hot days, Josh and Britton may take a refreshing dip in the creek. "It's mountain spring–fed, so it's pretty chilly," says Josh.

More often, the couple can be found hiking the trails near their property or attending a potluck dinner hosted by a neighbor. Potlucks are a blessing since neither cooks very often in San Francisco. Still, Britton admits that whenever he's at the creek, he feels compelled to whip up a big pot of stew—especially on damp days when he's inside watching the rain drip through the branches of the redwood trees.

NATURE'S OFFICE

Because both Josh and Britton are self-employed (Josh is a creative director/graphic designer and Britton is a market strategy consultant), they have the freedom to work remotely. Therefore, the couple spends much of their summers at the cabin.

"I might look up from my laptop and spot a mother deer and her fawn just across the creek," says Britton. "It sure beats the view from an office!"

Josh and Britton also see wild turkey, cheeping ducklings, and baby raccoons scouring the creek bed for crayfish and worms. One early morning, Britton peered out the window to find a bobcat sharpening its claws on a redwood tree. Startling, yes, but it's the swooping egrets that most often catch the owners by surprise.

"I'll be on the sofa and out of the corner of my eye, it looks like a white missile has flown by," says Britton.

A MAGICAL FRAMEWORK

The couple says that those who visit the original cabin are stunned when they see the revised masterpiece.

"They step into the living room and fall silent," says Josh, who thinks the reason it's so impressive is because the window's frame glorifies the landscape.

"It's funny," Britton says, "because the view can feel more impressive from the inside looking out than when you're actually standing outside amid nature!"

Inside or outside, winter or summer, rain or shine, this revamped creekside cabin is just what the owners had wanted—an intimate sanctuary.

"From my point of view," says Britton, "this place is magical." ∎

THE LEGACY CABIN

Legacy cabin stories are rooted in a strong sense of history and family. For some of the families, their new or restored cabins are a loving testimony to their ancestors and a multigenerational tradition of cabin living. Others built new cabins with the future in mind, looking forward to enjoying good times with their children, grandchildren, nephews, and nieces as they create new memories.

A New Jersey couple is living the good life on the Chain O' Lakes in Wisconsin.

"THE WHOLE THING IS ABOUT THE VIEW AND A RELAXED ATMOSPHERE."

DREAM REALIZED: RETIRING ON THE LAKE

The list of dream destinations for one's retirement years is familiar: Arizona, Florida, Texas . . . maybe a beach house in Mexico. But a lake home in east-central Wisconsin?

Well, Wisconsin won out for New Jersey residents Tom and Barbara. They set their sights on the Chain O' Lakes region near Waupaca. Why? The short answer is that their (grown) children made them an offer they could not refuse.

Retiring there was both a homecoming and the realization of a dream.

A FAMILY LEGACY

Barbara's family is deeply rooted in the Chain O' Lakes area, so named for its twenty-two interconnected lakes.

Since she was five years old, her parents established a family tradition of vacationing every year on the Chain O' Lakes. "No Disneyland for my family," she recalls. "We vacationed up north every year religiously, sometimes for a week, but up to a

The wall in the staircase is actually stone veneer.

From gardening to relaxing, this cabin has a lot to offer the retired couple.

month, and rented different places on the various lakes that make up the Chain O' Lakes, including Round, Columbia, Miner, and Rainbow."

Barbara and Tom met in 1967 at the University of Wisconsin–Milwaukee. That same year, Barbara introduced Tom to the Chain O' Lakes. While Tom didn't grow up with cabins, camping and nature were part of his Eagle Scout upbringing, and he was immediately enthralled with lake and cabin life.

In 1973, the couple married. They lived in Milwaukee until Tom's career took them to Cincinnati and then to New Jersey. The plan was to live in Jersey for a maximum of ten years.

THE LEGACY CONTINUES

Ten stretched into thirty. The couple raised daughters Nikki and Tami in Jersey. Still, the family returned to the Chain O' Lakes every summer for vacations.

The girls are grown now, with families of their own. Nikki lives in San Francisco with her husband, Ryan, and their son; Tami lives in Elizabethtown, Pennsylvania, with Steven and their daughter.

When Tom turned sixty-two years old, he was laid off; it was time to get serious about retirement plans. As Nikki and Tami listened to their parents weigh options, the daughters proposed their own plan. "They told us, 'If you want us to visit, you need to retire on the Chain O' Lakes,'" Barbara recalls with a laugh.

Decision made.

TEARING DOWN AND BUILDING UP

When the couple purchased property on Dake Lake they didn't rush into building. "We had about four years to go to log home shows, do research and compile ideas—of what we liked and

The home's logs are pine, while the floor is all hickory. The open ceiling contributes to a spacious feel.

In this lake home, it's the four-season room that everyone gravitates to.

The upstairs loft provides a sitting area for family time.

The deck looks out over the lake.

what we didn't like," Tom says. "We were living in New Jersey when we began construction, so the house was going up, and we came in during the construction about three times."

ONLY ONE THROAT TO CHOKE

When it came to buying their log package and hiring a builder, the couple went with Strongwood Log & Timber Homes. The Waupaca-based company is both a custom home builder and a log manufacturer. "Now I only had one throat to choke," Tom says with a chuckle.

Being local also meant that Strongwood was able to help Tom and Barbara navigate Waupaca's tight zoning restrictions and required setbacks from the water. "We have a narrow lot that's about 0.6 of an acre, and they [Strongwood] did a good job of using the property; the whole thing is about the view and a relaxed atmosphere," Tom says.

Barbara points to the patio on the lake side of her home and says, "That's as close as we could get to the lake with our patio. And on the sides of our house, the retaining walls had to be a certain way . . . It was kind of tricky."

Preparing the construction site was also tricky. In order to build, Strongwood had to drive 30-foot log pilings into the ground.

OPEN AND LIVABLE WITH GREAT SIGHT LINES

The design process was collaborative between the homeowners and Strongwood. "They designed around the property, and we gave a lot of input," notes Tom.

The couple ensured their dream home on the lake would serve them well in later years. "Basically, when we built the house, we knew it was going to be for retirement, so we wanted everything that we could on the first level so that

From their dock, the owners can venture out onto their lake and explore twenty-one other connected lakes.

we don't have to use the upstairs," Barbara says. And in case they need wheelchair accessibility some day, doorways are all an extra-wide thirty-six inches.

They also wanted an open-concept design. "It just worked out well because the view lets you see water on three sides, 180 degrees," says Barbara. She and Tom agree that their favorite part of their lake home is the four-season room with its six windows providing an excellent view of the lake. "We really like this, how it's bumped out instead of the wall going straight across," says Tom. "We worked with the builder on it. By having it angular, you can have more windows and a better, more panoramic view."

The couple made choices along the way to stay within budget, like choosing laminate countertops over granite. But they didn't scrimp on space in high-use areas since this is their primary home, not a vacation retreat. "We wanted a big kitchen so that we can entertain a lot," says Barbara. The kitchen also includes a sizable pantry. Tom

"WE LIKE TO JUST FLOAT AROUND IN THE LAKE TOGETHER LIKE OTTERS."

The placement of the fireplace means you can see both the fireplace and the lake from the great room, kitchen, and loft.

requested oversized dormers upstairs, which he estimates added about 600 square feet to the second floor.

In other areas, the couple economized on space. For instance, the washer and dryer are stacked in the mudroom. Tom's desk is built into a loft wall. And pocket doors were installed in the mudroom and the powder room.

ABOUT WOOD AND STONE

For décor choices, the couple's research binders served them well. "One thing we learned when compiling all these things was to not have too much wood in a log home. So most of our interior walls are drywall, so we can paint and change the color whenever we want to," says Barbara.

The log construction is pine, but the couple chose hickory for their hardwood floors. "A nice thing about hickory is that everything seems to go with it because it has so many different wood tones," says Barbara. The beautiful stone wall beneath the staircase was also her idea. "I had seen that in a magazine," she says.

THE GOOD LIFE

Pontoon boat tours through the Chain O'Lakes are a staple of life here. "We never get tired of it," Tom said. Their daughters Nikki and Tami visit with their families every summer. "We like to just float around in the lake together like otters," laughs Barbara. The gang floats near the dock on blow-up rafts, she says, "eating, drinking, sunbathing, talking, and singing songs."

"As much as we love summer and having the kids here, fall is gorgeous," adds Tom. "In October, we take the canoe to the upper chain, which consists of five lakes. It's pristine there—no motors, few homes. We bring a picnic basket, and it's just great," Tom said, beaming.

"It's like we're on a permanent vacation," agrees Barbara. "We never have to go anywhere because it's here. Everyone can come to us." ∎

This cabin may be small, but it's big on enjoyment for family and friends.

"IT'S NOTHING FANCY, AS IT STILL IS A CABIN."

RENOVATING A NORTHWOODS FAMILY TREASURE

Four generations have enjoyed what started as the "Mork Family Cabin" on O'Brien Lake in north-central Minnesota. Originally built in 1958 by Clarence (Cal) and Esther Mork, this cabin has provided special memories for countless friends and family. It even played a role in bringing together some couples, including current owners Jeff and Lindsay Balmer.

Jeff and his brother, Matt, are the Morks' grandsons. The brothers are also partners at Lands End Development, a design-build firm based in Crosslake, Minnesota. Matt is in charge of sales and marketing, while Jeff provides architectural design. It was a no-brainer that Lands End would serve as contractor for the cabin's renovation.

And about the cabin as matchmaker? Well, it's a familiar tale of young love played out since the dawn of cabin time: Lindsay was friends with Jeff and Matt's cousins. The kids gathered at the cabin for summertime fun, and young love blossomed.

A dresser and fish-theme mirror add charm to the bathroom.

Iconic elements of the original cabin were kept, such as Cal's boat on top of the blue cabinet.

THE ORIGINAL CABIN

The original 920-square-foot cabin was finished with cedar paneling and pine floors and had a living room, kitchen, bedroom, and sleeping loft. But it lacked a bathroom and electricity. To the delight of daughters Priscilla and Sarah, Cal added those "luxuries" in 1963, along with a screened porch overlooking the lake. While Esther would have gladly continued using kerosene lamps, having a "real" refrigerator meant the Morks didn't need to stop for ice en route to the cabin. (Back then, ice was harvested from Mille Lacs Lake in the winter; the blocks were stored in sawdust for the kitchen icebox.) But other than a well that was added, the seasonal cabin remained untouched by time.

THE BLEND OF OLD AND NEW

Not wanting to impinge on the memories or character of this small but special cabin, Jeff and Lindsay retained numerous iconic elements.

The blend of old and new woodwork continues the ties to the great Northwoods setting. All interior walls and ceiling coverings are cedar to match the original paneling. The original pine floors were not refinished at all. "They are well worn and a nod to how well-loved and used the cabin has been over the years," says Jeff. The stair railing and lighting boast a Scandinavian look to match the feel of the rest of the place.

The project got under way with the conversion of the unheated cabin to a year-round retreat. "We started by insulating the crawlspace walls and floor with spray foam insulation," recalls Jeff. Interior walls and ceilings were insulated as well—a fairly easy task, since the originals were just exposed studs and rafters. A furnace was installed and the mechanical systems updated. Single-pane windows were replaced with insulated glass, and new corner windows were added

The Scandinavian detail on the screen door adds to the cabin's whimsy.

If you host guests on summer weekends, consider adding an outdoor shower to free up the bathroom.

to maximize lake views. The Balmers redid the kitchen and expanded the master bedroom with a hundred-square-foot addition. The cabin now boasts a washer and dryer, along with a shower in the bathroom and another outdoors.

While the kitchen was part of the remodel, it showcases numerous elements from the former design. Originally, some of its walls were covered in pegboard for easy storage/hanging—today, one wall (now in the living room) still holds that handy pegboard. The ceramic kitchen sink evokes a nostalgic reaction from Sarah's daughter, Ginny

---

PAGES FROM TIME

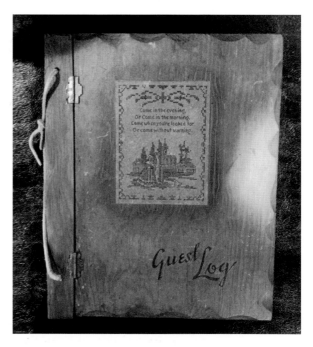

Soon after the original cabin was built in 1958, Cal Mork started a tradition—a visitors' journal, aptly named the "Guest Log." Highlighting family and friends' antics, it paints a vivid picture of time well-spent at the cabin. Take a leaf from Cal's book and start your own guest journal.

This sign translates to "Please enjoy—welcome."

The cabin offers great views of O'Brien Lake.

Janelle. "When I was a baby, my mom bathed me in the kitchen sink," says Ginny. "I have a picture of my daughter, Anna, taking a bath in the same sink that is still present in the renovated cabin."

Among other mementos from the old days are Cal's deer trophy, a model boat on top of the hutch, and the Dutch hex sign above the front door. After being married for 66 years, Cal passed away at the age of 101 in 2008. Unfortunately, he was unable to see his remodeled gem.

But his ingenuity is evident throughout. (Cal even repurposed a tuna can, which he painted red, to house the connection of the kitchen light to the ceiling. The light fixture still hangs—complete with tuna can.)

Cal's woodworking skills were definitely passed down to his grandsons. Jeff crafted the blue hutch in the living room as well as bedroom furniture, kitchen and bathroom

"WHEN I WAS A BABY, MY MOM BATHED ME IN THE KITCHEN SINK."

cabinets, and a corner booth for the original dining table. A whimsical bathroom mirror, along with exterior and screen doors are also his handiwork. "The décor is a bit of an eclectic mix of items that have been in the cabin for a long time, as well as new additions. It's nothing fancy, as it still is a cabin," Jeff says with affection.

COME JOIN US

The old cabin was a gathering spot, beckoning people to enjoy the quiet life and hospitality of the Morks. At the end of the driveway, a sign shaped like an old-fashioned coffee pot read "Var så god" as a nod to Cal and Esther's Norwegian heritage. The phrase has different meanings to Scandinavians, but at this cabin it meant "Please enjoy—welcome." And many people did come and enjoy this cabin. A journal, started in 1958 by Cal, chronicles the adventures of family and guests over the next fifty-four years. "It holds hundreds of fascinating entries and lake stories," says Matt Balmer. "Most entries were by folks telling of their stay and thanking my grandparents."

From the beginning, good times abounded: swimming, making fudge on rainy days, picking blueberries, and other familiar rites of summer. Rides on Cal's homemade pontoon boat—the first on the lake—were always an adventure. The Morks also hosted large family reunions. "I'm not sure how they fit, but they did," Sarah says. "I remember people sleeping all over the floor."

The third generation—Matt, Jeff, and their cousins Ginny and Mary—spent countless hours waterskiing, kneeboarding, and making items out of wood to tow behind the boat. Two old mini-bikes were commissioned for fun for when the kids were not in the water.

Now, *their* children spend countless hours engaged in the same water activities—minus the woodworking. Jeff even purchased a mini-bike. Sometimes the family ventures into the nearby town of Crosslake for treats at The Chocolate Ox, an old-fashioned candy store in the town square. On Saturday nights, people flock to the town square for the live music. "We often hit that and grab a pizza from Rafferty's Pizza, another of our favorite stops," says Jeff. "Crosslake is a small vacation town, where you know most of the people in the winter and very few in the summer! But it's a growing community as more people retire to their lakehomes."

The Balmers' cabin continues the family heritage—Var så god! ∎

The patio gives the owners room to expand and entertain in the summer, which is the busy time at the cabin.

The owner's wish list for her new retreat
included a cottage feel, lots of windows,
and nice finish materials.

TWENTY-FIVE YEARS IN THE MAKING

Benjamin Franklin once wrote, "He that can have patience can have what he will." Boy, did cabin owner Gayle Litchy have patience! After twenty-five years, she finally realized her dream of owning a cabin by the lake.

"I've had this dream for as long as I can remember," Gayle says. "I probably was influenced in large part by my parents' lake home, which they built in 1976." But Gayle's dream cabin wasn't going to come ready-made. "I've always had an interest in someday building a custom home. I really liked the idea of being able to figure out the spaces you want, the materials to use, and then finally decorating, all while trying to stay within a certain budget."

LOVE AT FIRST VIEW

After scouring many real estate circulars and checking out potential leads, she found the spot: just over an acre of land on Kimball Lake in central Minnesota. "I fell in love with the spectacular south-facing view because of the high elevation and the nice shoreline for swimming," says Gayle.

The biggest challenge was getting everything to fit into a small footprint. Three levels helped the owner get the spaces she wanted.

This sign reflects the owner's personal philosophy.

At the time, she worked in downtown Minneapolis and lived in a one-bedroom condo in the suburbs. Gayle often visited her land, nearly three hours from home, where she could indulge her gardening passion. "My parents have a lake home on North Long Lake [about twenty-five miles south], so I would often stay with them and just come up for the day."

Scrimping and saving over the years, she was able to build the beautiful 1,656-square-foot, two-bedroom retreat she now occupies as a retiree. "For the most part, I live at the lake, even though I still have my condo in New Hope and use it often, especially in the winter." The Twin Cities area is where her parents, most of her extended family, and many of her friends live. "It's easier for me to visit them than for them to come to the cabin in the winter," Gayle says.

DREAM CABIN

Work on the cabin began when she chose Lands End Development, a custom home designer and builder in nearby Crosslake, to bring the dream to life. "She wanted a real cottage feel," says Matt Balmer, who co-owns the firm with his brother, Jeff Balmer. "There are coffered ceilings, beadboard, natural wood, and just a blend of textures. Most of the materials were sourced locally, which helped keep costs down."

Gayle's wish list included "lots of windows, a fireplace, and nice finish materials." A bathroom on each the cabin's three floors was also a must.

DESIGN CHALLENGES

"The biggest challenge was getting everything to fit into the small footprint," adds Jeff Balmer. "But we enjoy those challenges."

Also figuring in the cabin's design was Gayle's love of nature. "I wanted to save a large red pine

Sleeping next to the window, you can hear the loons calling to each other and see the moon shining on the water.

Coffered ceilings, natural light, and an open floor plan were some of the must-haves for this dream cabin.

Having a bathroom on each floor was also on the "must-have" list.

The owner dedicated space above the garage for her hobbies.

"WE ENJOY SWIMMING, CRAFTING, PLAYING GAMES, AND SITTING BY THE CAMPFIRE."

tree that was in the middle of the buildable area," she said. "It worked out that the tree became the focal point between the house and garage."

Other site considerations included the fact that the property is on a bluff. "I was forced to build approximately 125 feet back from the lake and 30 feet back from the top of the bluff," Gayle says. Allowing space for the septic and well condensed Gayle's buildable space even more. However, she was undeterred. "I needed to keep the footprint small and use three levels to get the spaces I wanted. It worked out perfectly. So instead of worrying about the fact that I'm getting older and it might be harder to live on different levels, I look at it as a way to keep me fit. And I love the size, shape, and the way the house ended up sited on the property."

The building project had to take into account that the property is located on a bluff.

The 672-square-foot main floor features an open concept living room, dining area, and kitchen, along with half bath. A master suite lays claim to the second floor.

The walkout basement has a bedroom, a small family room, a laundry closet, bath, office nook, and mechanical room. "With the setback of Gayle's land on the knoll, we had to look at different layouts," says Jeff. "We worked in a reverse walkout where the walkout is toward the road rather than the lake."

Plus, Gayle wanted bonus space above the one-car garage. Two built-in beds, a sitting area, and a large table for crafting make good use of the extra 432 square feet. "I enjoy many, many crafts including making mosaics and baby quilts," she says.

LIVING AT THE LAKE

When not crafting, Gayle enjoys hiking, snowshoeing, and biking. "Mostly I love gardening and making my outside as beautiful as the inside," she says.

She also loves hosting family and friends at her retreat. Of special importance are her grand-nieces and grand-nephews. "We enjoy swimming, crafting, playing games, and sitting by the campfire," says Gayle. "The kids love sleeping in the window bed or in the upper garage, and the girls love my big freestanding bathtub."

This cabin definitely proves that good things come to those who wait. ∎

The owner wanted a rustic look for the outside of her cabin with an interior that has some fine homebuilding qualities.

Nestled between a rushing stream and a steep mountainside, the stone-sheathed family cottage stands on the footprint of the humble cabin built long ago by the homeowner's grandfather.

A CREEKSIDE COTTAGE FOR THE AGES

Hidden deep in the Pisgah National Forest of western North Carolina, the humble retreat was called the "Kibbin" because its owner's youngest son, aged three, could not pronounce "cabin."

A PLACE OF MEMORIES

The saga begins in the 1930s, when a local judge bought the property. The seller was "a young mountain man who planned to build a home for his fiancée," explains the judge's grandson and today's cabin owner, Larry. "But she left him and went to California, so my grandfather took the land and the timbers off the young man's hands for fifty dollars."

"We all have great family memories there," Larry continues. "The mountain was very high; the creek was very cold. As kids, we played in that creek, tucked up against that mountain. My grandfather also used the retreat as a connections place when he held 'Kibbin parties.' They became quite the tradition."

Over the objections of his grandchildren, the judge eventually sold the one-story wood cabin. But its memories continued to resonate. So when

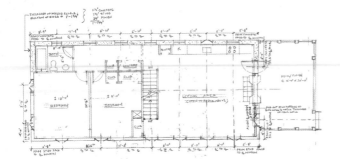

The main floor plan includes the new porch, which is accessed from the great room via a Dutch door.

A metal roof echoing the cottage's main roof shelters the front door.

the original Kibbin and seven surrounding acres came up for sale four decades later, Larry (by then, an attorney in Atlanta) was overjoyed. Wife Dana was more than a little relieved that Larry's long-held dream had come true. "For years, he would go by and leave his card in the door with a scribbled note asking for a call if they ever wanted to sell. The place has incredible meaning for him."

A CHALLENGING REBUILD

Thrilling as it was to own the Kibbin, the place was on its last legs. "There was no way to save it," notes John Altobello. The Cambridge, Massachusetts, architect came to know the home-owners when he designed houses for them in Atlanta and on Cape Cod. "They asked, 'Can we at least keep the site?' So we set out to create a new Kibbin on the exact spot of the original."

However, it was not an easy task. The building site occupied a sliver of land wedged between the creek rushing downhill and the mountainside rising up behind it. Altobello designed a long, narrow structure to fit the lot. The 50 by 22-foot cabin overlooks the creek. Crowned with a metal roof, its exterior is sheathed with stone from a local quarry. The inspiration came from Cotswold cottages the owners saw in England. "When we talked about the design, they sent me stacks of books with pictures of Cotswold stone houses," explains Altobello. "The stone on the Kibbin is, in fact, a face applied to a wood frame."

To build against the steep wall of the mountainside, Altobello designed a hefty retaining wall. It forms the back of the structure on the lower level "so that the mountain does not come sliding down into the water," the architect says. "It was the most challenging aspect of the design: how to make the house fit with a two-foot-thick retaining wall at ground level."

The designer
combined the
rustic sensibility of
a cabin with that
of a light and airy
Swedish home.

A barrel catches rain from one of the cabin's downspouts.

"Even though it's on seven acres, most of that acreage is forested and set at a fifty-plus-degree angle up to the ridgeline 170 feet above and behind the Kibbin," Larry explains. "We are so tight against the mountain that our builder, Larry Gibson of Clayton, Georgia, said that it was the hardest site he had ever worked with."

AN OPEN GATHERING PLACE

The lower floor of the 2,400-square-foot structure features a bathroom, a bedroom, and the utility areas. The main living space is on the upper level, where a vaulted great room encompasses a living room, a dining area, and a kitchen against one long wall. Curved trusses designed by Altobello support the great volume of open space. Furnished with clean-lined, traditional furniture, the room is oriented toward a large fireplace and a chimney built of the same stone that forms the building's exterior.

A vaulted ceiling gets support from structural timbers with decorative curves.

The dining area is cozy next to the fireplace.

The owners host many family meals on the screened porch until it gets too cold to sit outside.

"I wanted a room where everyone would be together," says Dana. "We all sit in that room, reading, talking."

At the fireplace end of the room, a Dutch door leads into a screened porch. This spacious indoor-outdoor room is also oriented around a stone fireplace. The back-to-back fireplaces share the chimney.

"We eat outside until it gets too cold," Dana says.

Also on this level is the master bedroom; a staircase leads to loft bedrooms.

"At first, we talked about installing a spiral staircase," Altobello says. "But we realized that it's not so easy to negotiate circular stairs with a basket of laundry in your arms. Instead, we decided to make stairs that are an architectural element. They also balance the big stone fireplace opposite."

"THE PLACE HAS INCREDIBLE MEANING FOR HIM."

Altobello's design places four tall windows on the great room walls. Additional light pours into the room via four skylights. "They line up with the big windows," he points out. "Natural light is very important to that big living space. There are also windows above the fireplace. The shutters opening to the great room from the upstairs loft are left open during the day, bringing light into that area."

FAMILY TIME

Larry and Dana come here for weekends, vacation, and holidays.

"I love that it's so remote; we have great family time here," Dana says.

Larry says that one of their year-round activities is to hike in the surrounding old-growth forest.

"But our very favorite thing to do," Larry adds with a smile, "is to sit on the porch and listen to the music of the creek." Now that is cabin living at its finest. ■

The great room fulfills the owners' desire to have a space where the whole family can gather.

This Maine cabin is enjoying its second life. Originally a Swedish pioneer's homestead cabin, it was rebuilt log by log by the pioneer's great-grandson and his wife.

REBUILDING A PIONEER CABIN

Driving along the narrow, sparsely wooded roads that lead to Maine's coast, roadside interests include makeshift berry stands, the odd sailboat for sale—even lichen-encrusted boulders from far-off lands dropped in by glaciers. But at the end of one finger of land stands something truly unexpected: a nineteenth-century, handhewn Swedish log cabin (with beginnings nowhere near its current site on the Gulf of Maine). The short answer of how it came to be there has something to do with the Homestead Act of 1862 and Maine's early self-promotion, but the longer answer is all about family.

REBUILDING A FAMILY LEGACY

It was there in 1888 that Carl Johnson arrived from "the old country." He is presumed to have built the cabin with the traditional steep roof and neatly dovetailed corners, which now overlooks Cundy's Harbor and Dingley Island.

"Carl Johnson was my great-grandfather," explains Greg Johnson. A trim, spectacled man in his sixties, Johnson looks relaxed in a pinstriped shirt and boat shoes on the cabin's screened-in

From their front porch, the owners have a view of an island where many families spend the summer.

It's a Swedish custom to put out a wheat sheaf in the winter for the birds to feed on.

porch. "And my grandfather and father were born here, too. Right over there," he says, gesturing toward a log wall of what is now the living area. "That was the birthing room."

Nearly a hundred years after the cabin's construction, it fell into disrepair from sitting vacant for decades. So it was disassembled, the logs carefully marked, and their wooden peg fasteners put in potato barrels. Then the whole thing was stored in a barn. And there it sat.

Greg and his wife, Joy, returned to their home state after years of living around the world during Greg's service as an admiral in the Navy. "By this time, my mother had moved to [nearby] Brunswick, and we started visiting her. Then this saltwater farm came up on the market . . ." Yes, they bought it. At their seaside farm, Greg and Joy keep forty chickens. He laughingly observes that the hobby "has not been a very good business model, but it is great fun and rewarding."

Ten years later, the Johnsons graded a field by the farm's inlet near the harbor for a plot on which to reconstruct the ancestral home.

SOMETHING OLD, SOMETHING NEW

The cabin was reconstructed in two phases. First, retired engineer Larry Totten (he designed Navy ships at the famed Bath Iron Works) tackled the initial design work. Larry reconfigured and expanded the original cabin to include a full basement, two additional bedrooms, and a gourmet kitchen. Then, using antique tools, he hewed the timbers into replicas. While the bottom logs aged, Larry assembled the rest of the cabin upside down. Lastly, he moved everything less than a quarter mile down the hill to the waterfront, one log at a time.

In traditional Swedish Christmas style, the Johnsons' tree is adorned with woven red-felt hearts, stars, and other ornaments woven from wheat straw.

The light fixture over the table is an antique from Sweden that's been updated with electricity.

The footprint of the original cabin was reconfigured to include this gourmet kitchen.

NEW SWEDEN

In the 1860s, newspapers buzzed with news of free land available to those willing to farm it. "Go West, young man" was the refrain, and people were doing just that, to the vexation of the already underpopulated state of Maine.

Soon after, then Maine Governor Joshua Chamberlain proclaimed, "If we cannot keep our sons at home, let us bring in our cousins," and dispatched a delegation to Sweden in search of industrious folks to farm the upper wilds of the state. Twenty-two men, eleven women, and eighteen children answered the call and formed "New Sweden," a colony in Maine's far northeast corner.

"The only things that went missing during that whole time were the potato barrels with the wooden pegs. We had to use 18-inch lag bolts instead." Greg adds. "Without Larry's craftsmanship and passion, we couldn't have gotten this project going."

Once stacked back together, the old hand-hewn logs were made weathertight after hours of caulking. "Here, we get driving northeast horizontal rains off the ocean," explains Greg. "Being watertight is important."

After the cabin was framed and assembled, it was time for the second phase of construction. In came builder Robert Moulton, of Bath, Maine, and his crew to do the finishing work.

"Both builders [Moulton and Totten] were creative and a pleasure to work with," recalls Greg.

"IT SEEMS THAT ALL OF THE GUESTS WE HAVE ENTERTAINED ALWAYS WANT A 'TOUR' OF THE CABIN AND A SUMMARY OF ITS HISTORY."

"It was really an awful lot of ad hoc design as we moved along. Joy was the creative spirit who made the construction project into a wonderfully warm home."

The updated cabin included the modern luxury of indoor plumbing and new flooring. "We wanted the floors to be pine, like the original, but Maine white pine is a very soft wood," explains Greg. "When I was an aviator in Jacksonville, Florida, we had heart-of-pine flooring. We decided that was more practical." This hard, durable, and all-reclaimed flooring has become a lasting contribution from the fourth generation of Johnsons in this cabin.

LIFE IN STYLE

The treasured cabin, now named "Farfar Stuga," which translates from Swedish as Grandfather's Cottage (or literally, Father's-Father's Cottage), is by no means a museum. Greg and Joy lived in the cabin for an entire year while their farmhouse was

The owner takes one of her grandsons for a carriage ride.

remodeled. "We were quite comfortable," he says. Unlike their ancestors, the couple enjoyed modern conveniences like in-floor radiant heat and a wood-burning Scan stove from Denmark.

The cottage's primary function, however, is to house overnight visitors. "It's a guesthouse and also a place to entertain," says Greg. Part of the experience is the cabin's history. "Over the past six years, it seems that all of the guests we have entertained always want a 'tour' of the cabin and a summary of its history."

And the extended family also recently held Greg's mother's birthday at the cabin. The celebration gathered many around favorite foods, including traditional rye bread made from her recipe.

But the best part of Farfar Stuga seems to be the couple's enjoyment of their adult children and grandchildren, whose names are stenciled high along the living room's walls between ceiling beams.

The young, blond boys enjoy gathering eggs from the farm chickens and, in the summer, pulling in the family's lobster traps from the bay with their grandfather. The Johnsons have a recreational license for lobstering. And how about the end result, come dinnertime? Greg, true to his Maine roots, proudly reports: "We have preparing [lobster] down to a science."

SWEDISH DÉCOR AND STYLE

Although the cabin has grown, one original aspect that remains honored is the detailed Swedish styling. "Much of it is based on the style of Swedish artist Carl Larsson," says Greg, who credits Joy for the cabin's authentic décor.

This includes the interior's simple whitewash over the ceilings and exposed beams that brings lightness to the space. Another nod to old-time Swedish architecture are the charming built-in bed cubbies and the traditional secret compartments. "These details aren't just authentic, they're fun, too," smiles Greg, pulling a perfectly obscured pine box from within the stairwell.

Also adding to the cabin's genuine feel are Scandinavian antiques and reproductions. As an example, Greg indicates the old light fixture featuring four folk dancers each holding a candle. "We found that on a trip to Sweden. It's an antique made for holding candles, but we had it electrified so the dancers now each hold a light." And the family's television is concealed in a nineteenth-century hand-painted Swedish cupboard.

The simplicity of traditional Nordic décor, with its clean lines, also gives the cabin a modern flair. Marrying old with new relaxes the space, making it easy to enjoy— which the Johnsons clearly do. ■

A bigger view of the kitchen and the loft above.

The cabin owner envisioned a home floating above it all in a modern glass tree house.

A LITTLE CABIN SOARS WITH INCREDIBLE VIEWS

If Mike and Linda Smith had a theme song, it would likely be "On the Road Again." As reps for several women's clothing lines, the couple logs hundreds of miles every year, crisscrossing a territory that includes Colorado, Wyoming, and their home base in Montana. "We could have lived anywhere, but we both liked Bozeman," says Linda. She and Mike decided a few years back they needed an off-the-beaten-trail retreat where they could kick back and really leave the road behind.

The Smiths were already familiar with Swan Lake, a semi-remote locale an hour's drive from Glacier National Park. "We'd visited with friends who owned waterfront property there," says Mike. "It's a small, pristine body of water surrounded in part by national and state forest land, so there's a limit to the number of residences that can be built there, which we saw as a real plus," he adds. So

Designing a cabin for a steep lot full of mature trees thirty feet above the lake is a tall task. To tackle the feat, the property owners turned to their architect, who also happens to be their son.

The owners enjoy paddling together on Swan Lake in their matching kayaks.

the Smiths soon found themselves searching for a lakeside lot.

When a steep site flanked by mature trees with 200 feet of shoreline came on the market, they did not hesitate. "The property was totally private with incredible views of the water and the mountains," says Linda. "It was just perfect for our needs."

SITE DICTATES DESIGN

Purchasing the land turned out to be the easy part. The Smiths quickly discovered that building a structure on the acre lot that dropped thirty feet to the lake would not be simple. To tackle the challenge, they enlisted their architect son, Reid Smith.

Reid soon determined the site would definitely dictate the design. "In order to maintain the privacy and views, we needed to place the house high up and hunker it into the hillside," he says. A contemporary structure with clean lines was the only way to establish optimal view corridors, Reid maintained. "Traditional cabins tend to be introverted, so I pushed early on not to go rustic, but my parents were a little apprehensive at first."

In keeping with the cabin's architecture, the décor is elegant and light.

Clerestory windows lead the eye up and out to views of the tree canopy. They also open to aid with ventilation.

The cabin lives beyond its 1,100 square feet due to the easy flow between the indoor living area and deck.

The rectangular vessel sink and faucet are part of the guest bathroom's contemporary flair.

LETTING GO OF RUSTIC

For Mike, who grew up in southern California, it was hard to let go of the idea of a little cabin in the woods. "From a conceptual standpoint, I envisioned something more rustic," he admits.

But Linda—whose childhood in Minnesota included annual summer forays to the primitive family cabin and swimming in Lake Superior—loved the idea of floating above it all in a modern glass tree house. "My parents and grandparents had these really spare cabins with outhouses and no electricity. I have lots of wonderful memories from that time, but I was happy to go with something more contemporary and convenient for our retreat," she says.

DRAMATIC PANORAMA

With a little nudging, Mike concurred. Reid got on with creating a simple utilitarian form crafted from local ledge stone, rough-sawn cedar lap siding, and a rusted Cor-Ten steel roof. "Upon approach, the house isn't very exciting, but when you get farther in and see how the building pushes out and up toward the lake, it's very dramatic," says Reid. He extended the interior timber-frame rafters outside for additional effect.

A carefully conceived deck both expands the living space and continues the contemporary theme. "We used a minimalist steel railing to complement the architecture without impeding the panorama," he adds.

THE INTERIOR: SMALL SPACE LIVING LARGE

Inside, the 1,100 square feet lives large thanks to ceiling heights that go from nine feet in the kitchen to a soaring twelve feet in the main living area. The ascending fir ceiling tops stone walls that bookend the space; durable concrete floors handle wet flip-flops and snowy boots with equal ease.

At the center, a bank of windows wraps around to meet stone on either side. The biggest expanse of glass was placed front and center to frame the mountain and lake tableau. "The largest pane is at eye level, and there are smaller units above and below

The cabin owners' granddaughter has a great view while arranging flowers.

for ventilation," says Reid. "And because the house is built into the hillside, the cool earth provides air-conditioning."

With such a simple material palette outside, Mike and Linda opted for a similar approach indoors. But simple doesn't have to be boring. "It's not very fancy, but we wanted it to be fun so we added lots of color," says Linda, noting many of their selections were in direct response to the surrounding environment. "We chose those lime green dining room chairs because we see that color outside, and the painted turquoise backsplash in the kitchen references the lake. The orange bar stools are just for fun."

Frameless bamboo cabinets provide a quiet kitchen backdrop. To prevent the double-height island from looking too sleek, Reid mixed black granite on one end with a raised slab of reclaimed wood on the other. "I thought using an old bar top for one section made it more casual and approachable," he says. "This is Montana, after all."

Reid collaborated with his mother on the suspended cable lighting system that provides a glow when the sun goes down. "We didn't want recessed cans because it's not very energy efficient to punch holes in the ceiling," he says. "This was a way to create good, adaptable lighting that fits with the architecture."

In the master bedroom, soothing blues and browns mimic the hues in the stacked stone wall.

And, like the adjacent living room, the sleeping quarters enjoy spectacular vistas. "We can have snow until mid-July and can actually see the glacier from our bed," says Linda. Wildlife sightings are a regular phenomenon in their neck of the woods as well. "We've observed a bald eagle migration and have even seen a moose swimming across the lake."

In such tight quarters, storage is always at a premium. So in lieu of space-hogging doors and closets, Reid introduced bamboo built-ins in the master bathroom. "It's so much easier to pack and repack with this kind of storage setup," he says.

No strangers to living out of a suitcase, Mike and Linda appreciate those little amenities on their ever-increasing visits to Swan Lake. "We've started coming here in every season, but summer is still the big draw," says Mike. "We just wish the summer months were longer."

BIG-SKY LIVING

At least summer days seem to last forever. "It's not unusual for us to be on the lake until ten o'clock at night," says Linda, adding that a typical day starts with a morning hike or bike ride. "There's a southerly breeze in the morning, so the lake isn't always smooth, but by mid-afternoon it's perfect for kayaking."

The Smiths have two grown sons; when the kids and grandkids come to visit, there's a king-size pullout in the living room for those who like cushier accommodations, and a flat grassy spot outside for those who prefer to pitch a tent. "Our granddaughters love to

With a view like this, it might be hard to get out of bed in the morning.

camp, but everyone comes back here for meals," says Linda. "We enjoy lots of breakfast parties on the deck, and the dock is another living area, too."

Come evening, everyone heads down to the lake and boards the Smiths' twenty-one-foot Sea Ray. Most nights, they meet up with neighbors and tie their boats together. "Then we have cocktails and float for hours," says Linda. Mike adds, "The sunsets are magnificent."

If there's one time everyone in the Smith clan can agree upon for a family gathering, it's the Fourth of July. According to Mike, that's when one of their neighbors puts on a firework display that beats the city of Bozeman's show by a mile. "It's something we all look forward to, and there are somewhere between seventy-five and a hundred boats out for the celebration," he says. "A full moon and fireworks on the water. It doesn't get much better than that." ■

"WE CAN HAVE SNOW UNTIL MID-JULY AND CAN ACTUALLY SEE THE GLACIER FROM OUR BED."

A 1940s ski cabin gets transformed into a modern-day eco-friendly retreat.

FAMILY AFFAIR

Molly Breen had more than skiing on her mind when she went hunting for a ski cabin near Donner Lake with her husband, Mike McRae. "My daughter and her husband were living in Colorado and were talking about getting a cabin there. I thought if we got one here we could lure them back," Molly confesses.

She found the perfect bait: an old summer cabin atop Donner Summit in California's Sierra Nevada range. Located across the street from Royal Gorge (claimed to be North America's largest cross-country skiing resort), the cabin is just a forty-five-minute drive from home in Nevada City, California.

"I wanted for us to be able to walk out the door and ski, and it doesn't get much better than this," Molly says.

According to her daughter, Mela Breen, the plan worked—sort of. "My husband and I had decided to move back to our hometown anyway because I was pregnant with our first child, and we wanted to live close to our parents," says Mela. She's a LEED AP designer (and backcountry skier), and her husband, David Good, is a builder. The couple had just launched their own design/

The owners of this remodeled ski cabin used a sustainable approach when renovating it.

This bathroom reflects a clean, simple, uncluttered aesthetic.

build firm when the economy took a bad turn, and they found themselves with extra time. Both were enlisted to aid in the redesign. "Six weeks after our first son was born, we moved into a little rental cabin next door and started construction," she adds.

Mela and David ultimately spent six months working on the ailing 1940s structure, along with Molly and Mike..

CABIN UPGRADE

"It had no insulation, single-pane windows, and two woodstoves and a fireplace all in the same room," recalls Molly. She and Mike braved two winters visiting the 30 x 50-foot rectangular structure; they stoked the fire and thawed frozen pipes in between checking out the area's considerable Nordic skiing opportunities. "We wanted a slightly bigger, energy efficient, year-round getaway with enough space to accommodate three generations."

Mela and David reviewed the fairly extensive laundry list of considerations and tackled the project from the outside first to address the challenge of the elements. "Due to some of the heaviest snow loads in the country [the area averages thirty feet of snow a year], the existing cabin was being slowly crushed by the weight of the snow and was seven inches out of level," says Mela, who had the building leveled and a new foundation put under it.

The porch floor
incorporates
one of the
boulders that
accent the yard.

Built-in bed nooks can be found on the second floor.

A small play area is tucked under the eaves.

CONTINUING THE LEGACY

For those who have inherited a family cabin: lucky you! When passing down a cabin to the next generation, you might want to follow the example of the owners in this story. "We created a building that would use as little energy as possible so it would still be affordable in years to come, even as energy costs increase," says Mela, the owner's daughter and cabin remodeler. "The owners want to leave a cabin to their children and grandchildren with the knowledge that it would be sustainable for future generations."

The interior gutting and requisite demolition work fell to the older generation. "It's kind of an obsessive hobby of mine," says Molly, noting the five homes she's worked on before for herself. "My family says we specialize in demolition because I like to buy houses and take them to the dump."

With the heavy lifting done, Mela and David reconfigured the space, built a 265-square-foot addition, and expanded the total living area to a more commodious 1,800 square feet. They also provided an energy retrofit that included air sealing, insulation, and new windows.

"It was important to the owners [mother and stepfather] to create a building that would use as little energy as possible, and that meant a well-insulated envelope," says Mela. The roof was insulated with 3.5 inches of closed-cell spray foam with sprayed-in fiberglass underneath to create a high R-value roof assembly. The crawl space was sealed and the walls were insulated with sprayed-in fiberglass. During the remodel, particular attention was paid to air sealing and thermal bridging. A mechanical ventilation system was installed to provide a small amount of continuous fresh air so that the rooms don't get stuffy when the house is packed with guests. "When a building is this tight, you want to be sure and bring in fresh air."

A forced-air heating system keeps propane use down to around 500 gallons a year, and a condensing boiler on-demand hot water system warms water as needed rather than wasting energy to maintain a high temperature.

Dan Guyer, Mela's father, helped Dave frame the addition and plumbed the entire building. "My parents are still very good friends, and we are a tight family, so it was great having my dad's help on the project," says Mela.

INTERIOR AESTHETIC

All those involved agreed that the cabin should have a clean, modern look. The newly pitched roof provides the perfect opening statement. "My personal aesthetic tends toward contemporary, but I never do anything just for looks. There's often twenty feet of snow out there, and we needed a covered entry," says Mela. Regarding materials, everyone adopted a recycle and reuse sustainable philosophy. Mela used salvaged metal

This is the front of the ski retreat. Since the area sees a lot of snow, a covered entryway was deemed necessary.

The family collected items from many different sources to decorate their skiing retreat. But the pieces sit well together in this open space.

siding and timbers on the exterior. The porch ceiling boards were fashioned from interior wall sheathing removed during the remodel; railings are constructed from reclaimed steel panels.

The sustainability theme continues inside, where the living room's maple floors were cut from an old gym floor. The kitchen Marmoleum (a brand of linoleum), upper-level cork floors, and maple plywood cabinets were also environmentally conscious choices. "Whenever possible, we used recycled materials and bought things from local vendors," says Mela.

On any given weekend, as many as eight people pile into the compact space, making a workable floor plan paramount to the redesign. "The addition allowed for a larger kitchen and a third bedroom upstairs," says Mela, who created a gear/mudroom for hanging wet ski clothes and for dealing with the family's considerable collection of boots, skis, and other outdoor accoutrements. On the second floor are sleeping nooks, cozy play spaces for the grandkids, and enough room for multiple guests to pile in on powder days.

The carefully conceived kitchen—a mother/daughter collaboration—started with Molly's mandate for raised windows. "I lived there for two winters and saw how the snow covered the existing windows, and I wanted to be able to see out all the time, not just six months out of the year," she says.

Mela filled in with a mix of counter heights and surfaces, including EcoTop (a blend of recycled paper and bamboo) on the perimeter, butcher block on the island, and a stainless steel bar fashioned from an old restaurant table for additional food prep and casual dining. "The space was designed to be wide enough so several people could be in there at the same time," she says.

Molly had energy efficiency on the brain when she designed the kitchen's three-layer lighting system in accordance with California lighting standards. "There's a combination of incandescent light fixtures, florescent cans, and under-cabinet LED strips," she says. Two existing "funky chandeliers" were saved from the original structure to light the main bedroom and the entrance to the bunkroom at the top of the stairs.

SURROUNDING AREA

While the new digs get high marks, the main attraction remains the great outdoors. Skiing of all varieties is available nearby; a shuttle to the Sugar Bowl downhill area is just steps from the cabin.

But everyone seems to have his or her own motivation for showing up. Mike enjoys the mountain biking possibilities. Molly's other daughter, Susannah, is a triathlete who prefers the summer months when she can train at 7,200-foot altitude. Molly herself favors fall, when she enjoys the solitude of sculling on Donner Lake. "I like to get down there at first light when it's just me and a couple of fishermen," she says.

It's during those moments that she contemplates not just the beauty of her surroundings, but the pleasure in having created something that will stand the test of time. "This is going to be a place that my grandsons can enjoy, and hopefully their families after them." ■

CREDITS

Page ii: from "An Outdoorsy Little River Cabin," photo courtesy Bizios Architect

Page vi: from "A Cabin Built for Relaxation," photo by Greg Page Studios

Page vii (top): from "Dream Realized," Photo by Glen Sanderson

Page vii (bottom): from "A Cabin Designed for Prime Views," photo by Rob Karosis

Page viii: from "The Waiting Game," photo by Heidi A. Long

Page 5: from "The Waiting Game," photo by Heidi A. Long

Page 55: from "A Cabin Designed for Prime Views," photo by Rob Karosis

Pages 114–115: from "Cozy Meets Rustic," photo by Roger Wade, courtesy Hearthstone Homes

Page 147: from "Cabin in the Hills," photo by Mehosh Dziadzio Photography

Page 197: from "A Creekside Cottage for the Ages," photo by Todd Bush Photography, courtesy John Altobello

Page 256: from "Cozy Mountain Cabin," photo by Heidi A. Long

HEAVEN HAS A DOCK

Story by Julie Kuczynski
Photos by Hoffman Photography, courtesy Tomahawk Log & Country Homes
Builder: Tomahawk Log & Country Homes

A CABIN BUILT FOR RELAXATION

Story by Christy Heitger-Ewing
Photos by Greg Page Studios
Builder: Pioneer Log Homes Midwest

HILLSIDE HEAVEN

Story by Fran Sigurdsson
Photos by Kevin Meechan
Architect: Thomas Lawton, Architect AIA LEED AP

BLENDING VINTAGE & NEW

Story by Sarah Pinneo
Photos by Rob Karosis
Architect: Smith & Vansant Architects
Builder: G.R. Porter & Sons Custom Builders

THE WAITING GAME

Story by Stacy Durr Albert
Photos by Heidi A. Long
Log provider: Natural Log Creations
Builder: Bruce Jungnitsch

A BOYHOOD DREAM COMES TRUE

Story by Christy Heitger-Ewing
Photos by Heidi A. Long
Log provider: Kalispell Montana Log Homes
Interior design: Grizzly Interiors

BARNWOOD BEAUTY

Story by Christy Heitger-Ewing
Photos by Rick Hammer, courtesy Lands End Development
Design/Build: Lands End Development

SUMMER CAMP REVISITED

Story by Nancy E. Oates
Photos by Peter Montanti, Mountain Photographics, Inc.
Architect: Johnson Architecture, Inc.
Interior design: Blackberry Farm Design

FLOATING CABIN

Story by Gina Chiodi Grensing
Photos courtesy Rich & Marla Thomas
Remodeler: Cabin owners

AN OUTDOORSY LITTLE RIVER CABIN

Story by Christy Heitger-Ewing
Photos courtesy Bizios Architect
Architect: Bizios Architect

A CABIN DESIGNED FOR PRIME VIEWS

Story by Lucie B. Amundsen
Photos by Rob Karosis
Architect: Smith & Vansant Architects

FROM SOMETHING OLD TO SOMETHING NEW

Story by Christy Heitger-Ewing
Photos by Rick Hammer, courtesy Lands End Development
Design/Build: Lands End Development

THE AFFORDABLE LOG CABIN

Story by Mark R. Johnson
Photos by Rendulich Photography
Styling by Kristi Portugue & Carol M. Johnson
General contractor: Evergreen Construction

COZY MEETS RUSTIC
Story by Nancy E. Oates
Photos by Roger Wade, courtesy Hearthstone Homes
Styling by Debra Grahl
Builder: Hearthstone Homes

WHAT MORE DO YOU NEED?
Story by Melissa Mylchreest
Photos by Heidi A. Long
Log provider: Logcrafters Log & Timber Homes
Builder: Randy Baker

COZY MOUNTAIN CABIN
Story by Melissa Mylchreest
Photos by Heidi A. Long
Builder: J Martin Builders

THINK SMALL
Story by Debra Grahl
Photos by Roger Wade
Timber producer: British Columbia Timberframe Co.
Builder: Rebbecca Abair

A COMFY NORTHWOODS GETAWAY
Story by Christy Heitger-Ewing
Photos by Rick Hammer, courtesy Lands End Development
& BeDe Design
Design/Build: Lands End Development
Interior design: BeDe Design

SURFSIDE COTTAGE
Story by Nancy E. Oates
Photos by Terry Pommett Photography
Architect: Lisa Botticelli, Botticelli & Pohl Architects

WELCOME BACK
Story by Kristin Sutter
Photos by Tim Murphy, Fotoimagery.com
Architect: Peter Weber, Coburn Development, Inc.
General contractor: Mountain Home Construction

DIY CABIN REMODEL
Story by Melissa Mylchreest
Photos by Heidi A. Long
Remodeler: Cabin owners

CABIN IN THE HILLS
Story by Melissa Mylchreest
Photos by Mehosh Dziadzio Photography, www.mehosh.com
Remodeler: Cabin owner

A RUSTIC CABIN GETS A DRAMATIC UPDATE
Story by Christy Heitger-Ewing
Photos by Eric Rorer Photography, courtesy Amy A. Alper, Architect
Architect: Amy A. Alper, Architect

DREAM REALIZED: RETIRING ON THE LAKE
Story by Mark R. Johnson
Photos by Glenn Sanderson
Builder: Strongwood Log & Timber Homes

RENOVATING A NORTHWOODS FAMILY TREASURE
Story by Gina Chiodi Grensing
Photos by Rick Hammer, courtesy Lands End Development
Design/Build: Lands End Development

TWENTY-FIVE YEARS IN THE MAKING
Story by Gina Chiodi Grensing
Photos by Rick Hammer, courtesy Lands End Development
Design/Build: Lands End Development

A CREEKSIDE COTTAGE FOR THE AGES
Story by Regina Cole
Photos by Todd Bush Photography, courtesy John Altobello Architecture
Architect: John Altobello Architecture
Interior Design: Kathleen Wallace

REBUILDING A PIONEER CABIN
Story by Lucie B. Amundsen
Photos by Todd Caverly
Builder: Larry Totten

A LITTLE CABIN SOARS WITH INCREDIBLE VIEWS
Story by Mindy Pantiel
Photos by Roger Wade
Styling by Debra Grahl
Architect: Reid Smith Architects
Builder: SBC Construction

FAMILY AFFAIR
Story by Mindy Pantiel
Photos by Kat Alves Photography
Design/Build: Atmosphere Design Build